T0159013

The Comforting Whirlwind

The Comforting Whirlwind
God, Job, and the Scale of Creation

Bill McKibben

Cowley Publications
Cambridge, Massachusetts

Published in the United States of America by Cowley Publications, a division of the Society of Saint John the Evangelist. No portion of this book may be reproduced, stored in or introduced into a retrieval system, or transmitted, in any form or by any means—including photocopying—without the prior written permission of Cowley Publications, except in the case of brief quotations embedded in critical articles and reviews.

Library of Congress Cataloging-in-Publication Data

McKibben, Bill.
    The comforting whirlwind : God, Job, and the scale of creation / Bill McKibben.
        p. cm.
    Includes bibliographical references.
    ISBN-10: 1-56101-234-3 ISBN-13: 978-1-56101-234-3
        (pbk. : alk. paper)
    1. Bible. O.T. Job—Criticism, interpretation, etc. I. Title.
    BS1415.52.M35 2005
    223'.106—dc22
                                                    2005012075

Quotations from *The Book of Job*, translated and with an introduction by Stephen Mitchell, copyright © 1979 by Stephen Mitchell. Revised edition copyright © 1987 by Stephen Mitchell. Reprinted by permission of HarperCollins Publishers.

Cover design: Brad Norr Design

This book was printed in the United States of America on acid-free paper.

Second Printing

Cowley Publications
4 Brattle Street
Cambridge, Massachusetts 02138
800-225-1534 • www.cowley.org

For the men, women, and pastors of the
Johnsburg United Methodist Church

Contents

PREFACE

The 2004 presidential election contained, by most accounts, more "religion" than any campaign in the Republic's history. The victorious GOP attributed much of their success to organizing in the suburban megachurches of the swing states; polling showed that many Americans said they were "voting their values" by supporting the Bush administration. The Republicans have clearly emerged as the party of "faith"; even now the Democrats are sputtering in an effort to retool so they too can claim the mantle of religion.

But the very same people elected as guardians of moral values show up at the bottom of the list when it comes to protecting the environment: Show me a congressman with a perfect rating from the Christian Coalition and I will bet you he barely registers on the scorecard of the League of Conservation Voters.

I have been puzzled most of my life by this contradiction: How can one believe deeply in God and yet be so cavalier about God's creation?

I am by training a writer and an environmentalist, and by coincidence a Methodist Sunday school teacher. I'm not a professional theologian, nor even really an amateur. But I've wandered often through the Bible, stopping more and more frequently at the book of Job—a book that offers, I think, a radical, deeply biological, intensely exhilarating view of the meaning of our lives.

Job has been read many ways, of course. But like the rest of the Bible its exquisite environmental relevance has been generally overlooked. Now we need those stories. The relationship between people and their environment, which in the largest sense we could always take for granted, has suddenly begun to fray. To fray so badly, in fact, that most of us feel deep down as if our half-hearted responses—our recycling, our composting—are not as radical as the times demand.

The stories from the Bible—the answers from Job—are deeply radical; they will not fit comfortably with our present way of seeing things. Parts of these stories will be equally unpalatable to the left and to the right, and simply maddening to the middle. Still, the crisis—both physical and spiritual—in which we find ourselves is so deep that we will soon be turning in every direction for answers. I want to outline one of those possibilities, on the theory that the Bible still has some standing in our society—that an argument for deep change that summons the majesty of the wisdom literature may reach deeper inside us than the next fund-raising appeal for the Audubon Society.

I would like to thank several people for their help with this project. Molly Longstreth, Newell Wert, and especially Len Sweet invited me to give the 1992 Heck Lectures at United Theological Seminary in Dayton. This book was drawn from those lectures, and I am as grateful for their intellectual help as for their hospitality. I am not a lecturer by trade, and I have since revised my remarks extensively, incorporating chunks of both argument and text from my books *The End of Nature* and *The Age of Missing Information*, both originally published by Random House. The men and women of the Johnsburg United Methodist Church, and of Troy Conference of the United Methodist Church—in particular Lucy Hathaway, Barb Lemmel, Mitch Hay, Carol Anne Grieg, and Sabine O'Hara—have been inspirations. I am grateful to Stephen Mitchell for allowing me to quote at length from his splendid translation of the book of Job. Jon Pott has been more than patient waiting for my thoughts to coalesce; Gloria Loomis has been glorious as always; and Sue Halpern, my wife, and Sophie, my daughter, have made me better able to see the wonder of the world around.

CHAPTER

1

Job, as many have remarked before me, is not the story of a patient man. It is the immediately familiar and very modern story of a frustrated man, up against an orthodoxy that he no longer can believe in, but surrounded by a society that continues to insist that its accustomed interpretation is the only truth.

His problem is not only that he suffers—it is that he suffers without understanding why. To give the briefest of synopses, the prosperous Job suddenly finds his fortune gone, his children dead, and himself residing on a dung heap at the edge of town where he fills his hours picking at his innumerable scabs and running sores. In Stephen Mitchell's marvelous translation, he says:

> Each day I live seems endless,
>   and I suffer through endless nights.
> When I lie down, I long for morning;
>   when I get up, I long for evening;
>   all day I toss and turn.
> My flesh crawls with maggots;
>   my skin cracks and oozes.
> My days fly past me like a shuttle,
>   and my hope snaps like a thread.

This sorry man had three friends—Eliphaz, a Temanite, Bildad, a Shuhite, and Zophar, a Namathite. Hearing of his misfortune, they journeyed to Job so that they could comfort him. And they were good friends—when they first met him, they cried out, tore their clothes, and sprinkled dust on their heads. They even stayed silent for seven days and seven nights, awed in the face of this great suffering.

Finally, however, they began to talk. Their talk, and Job's answering soliloquies, fill twenty-nine chapters. It is unlike almost any other story in the Bible, where kingdoms tend to rise and fall in a single paragraph, eras begin and end with great economy, cataclysmic events come and go three and four to a page. Instead, it repeats and backtracks and rehashes chapter after chapter of the same arguments at a higher and higher pitch. It reminds me most of the daily in-and-out of a newspaper op-ed page, where some issue like the death penalty is examined day after day, year after year, till everyone knows all the arguments and has long since made up his or her mind. Bildad and Eliphaz and Zophar are the syndicated columnists of their day, repeating the old truths ad infinitum, though with considerably more literary flair. Their arguments hardly develop—they simply repeat the same wisdom of the ages, over and over again. As the liberation theologian Gustavo Gutierrez, who has written a fascinating book titled *On Job*, writes, "The author of this book may be trying to tell us by this wearisome repetition . . . that their theology is an exhausted mine and that it keeps turning in place like a serpent biting its own tail. The only thing that changes in their speeches is the tone, which becomes steadily more hostile and intolerant."

In any event, their calculus is simple: God is just, and therefore Job suffers because he is guilty. He has committed some sin.

Zophar says, "If God were to cross-examine you / and turned up your hidden motives / and presented his case against you / and told you why he has punished you— / you would know that your guilt is great." According to Eliphaz,

> Your guilt must be great indeed;
>> your crimes must be inconceivable.
> You cheated your dearest friends,
>> stripped your debtors naked,

stole food from the hungry,
> let the destitute starve,
spat on widow and orphan,
> laughed in the beggar's face.
That is why pain surrounds you
> and sudden terror has struck you.
Light is turned to darkness,
> and the waves close over your head.

It is, they concede, remotely possible that Job himself was not such a bad man—but in that case it was clearly his children who had messed up and landed their dad on the manure pile. As Bildad impatiently snorts at the end of one of Job's speeches:

How long will you go on ranting,
> filling our ears with trash?
Does God make straightness crooked
> or turn truth upside down?
Your children must have been evil:
> he punished them for their crimes.

The rigorously orthodox interpretation of the friends is justified by ancient usage—"It is the tradition of the sages who have remained faithful to their ancestors," says Eliphaz, that the wicked man writhes in pain all his days. It is the classic example of the conventional wisdom, that thing which everyone believes because it has been repeated to them a thousand times until it "just seems obvious."

Of course, like all conventional wisdom, it has a whole body of evidence to back it up. Or pseudo-evidence, since people rarely look into it, any more than they examine the modern-day legend of, say, "welfare cheats." Job's friends stress with complete assurance that every observation of the world around them coincides with their explanation. "Can an innocent man be punished? / Can a good man die in distress?" asks Eliphaz. "He speaks from experience; those who plow iniquity and sow disaster reap just that." God "traps the wise in their cleverness / and ruins the plots of the cunning," insists Eliphaz. God, adds Bildad, *never* "betrays the innocent / or takes the hand of the wicked. But "the righteous blossom in sunlight, / and the garden is filled with their seeds. / Their roots twine around stones / and fasten even to rocks," unlike the evil man, who "though he props up his house it collapses; / though he builds it again, it falls." Round after round they keep up their argument, heightening their hyperbole with each speech:

> The wicked man's life is a torment;
>> his days are anguish and pain.
> In his ear is the voice of terror;
>> in his mouth is the taste of death.
> He flees from darkness to darkness;
>> he is marked for the edge of the sword.
> His body is food for vultures;
>> disaster nibbles his flesh.
> Anguish pounds at his mind;
>> fear and panic assault him,
>> like a soldier before a battle.

Evil always catches up to its perpetrators, adds Zophar. "Though crime was sweet on his lips / and evil melted in his mouth, / though he tried to keep its flavor / and hold its taste on his tongue, / the food that he swallowed turns / to poison inside his belly."

This pious orthodoxy is the baseline for the entire story—it is the seemingly sturdy and immense castle that Job and God will totally demolish with the explosive force of their encounter at the end of the book.

Even as the story begins, though, the castle is beginning to fall apart, to look less and less imposing. And the reason is—Job has a new fact. He has a fact at odds with the conventional wisdom mouthed by his friends. His fact is this: he is not particularly guilty. In fact, he is innocent. "While there is life in this body," he tells his friends, "I will never let you convict me; / I will never give up my claim. / I will hold tight to my innocence; / my mind will never submit." He goes on to defend his conduct at great length:

> I brought relief to the beggar
>> and joy to the widow's heart.
> Righteousness was my clothing,
>> justice my robe and turban.
> I served as eyes for the blind,

> hands and feet for the crippled.
> To the destitute I was a father;
>   I fought for the stranger's rights. . . .
> If my loins were seduced by a woman
>   and I loitered at my neighbor's door—
> let any man take my wife
>   and grind in between her thighs! . . .
> If I ever neglected the poor
>   or made the innocent suffer;
> if I ate my meals alone
>   and did not share with the hungry;
> if I did not clothe the naked
>   or care for the ragged beggar; . . .
> let my arm fall from my shoulder
>   and my elbow be ripped from its socket!

And yet, undeniably, he is being treated like a villain. So if an all-powerful God exists (which for Job is a given), then the only conclusion must be that the orthodoxy is wrong. He doesn't want to believe this—"Isn't disgrace for sinners / and misery for the wicked?" he asks plaintively in his final summation. "Can't he tell right from wrong / or keep his accounts in order?" But he is an honest man—he cannot pretend he has been wicked, and so his mental world comes apart. "Why do the wicked prosper?" he asks his friends in a moment of seditious daring—he knows they will be appalled to hear him say it and will clap their hands to their mouths. "When I think of it I am terrified / and horror chills my flesh." But it is the truth. The wicked "live to a ripe old age" and "their children stand beside them; / their grandchildren sit on their laps." None of their bulls are impotent, and their cows don't miscarry, and their grandchildren skip about like lambs to the drum and lyre. "Haven't you talked with travelers?" he shouts at the friends. "Don't you know from their tales / that the sinner escapes destruction / and is spared on the day of wrath?"

The conventional wisdom is never routed so easily, of course. The tales of travelers or authors or prophets can usually be ignored. Maybe they don't know the whole story, maybe they are overreacting, maybe they are looking at too small a sample or for too short a time. In this case, though, the victory over the conventional wisdom is absolute, even before God appears in the whirlwind to scorn the arguments of Eliphaz, Bildad, and Zophar. We know from the very first lines of the book that in fact Job *is* innocent, that his torment has nothing to do with any sins and results instead from a silly wager between God and the devil. He has not deluded himself that he is not a sinner; his blamelessness is not open to interpretation, nor can it be shrugged off as unknowable. He's clean. It's like a movie where you know who the murderer is—the best arguments by the prosecutor as he tries to convict the innocent man fall flat because of the evidence of your eyes. He's not guilty. His innocence destroys the syllogism of the three friends, who in fact have been set up to look foolish.

A new fact in the world is a powerful thing. If it is a large enough fact, it can explode even the most patiently built-up and jealously guarded orthodoxy. The history of science is, of course, the best example. Since everyone knew that the earth was at the center of the universe, just as everyone knew that God rewarded the just, an elaborate conventional wisdom evolved to prove the point. Between Aristotle's crystalline spheres and Ptolemy's epicycles and the endless refinements of the medieval monks, the proof worked just well enough to sustain the belief. Copernicus introduced a new fact—that the system worked with much more elegance, and was much closer to the observations of astronomers, if the sun was placed at the center and the earth was placed in motion. With the new observations of Tycho and Kepler and others, it proved too large a fact to accommodate within the old system of thought, which thereupon crumbled.

By the end of the book of Job, we will have arrived at such a new paradigm, one that fits much closer the observed evidence of the world around us. It is, I think, a magnificent new vision of God and people, one with as much to offer us as Job. Much of this book will be taken up with a discussion of that new paradigm.

But in the meantime I want to back away from Job for a moment and show that we too live in the grip of conventional wisdoms that no longer fit easily with the observable facts.

* * *

If you turn on the news tonight, chances are you will hear an anchorperson say something like: "Good news on the economic scene tonight—according to the Federal Reserve, America's gross national product shot up by two percent in the second quarter of the year." Or "There are promising signs that car sales are beginning to accelerate." Or "New home construction is finally starting to rise, a move economists applauded as another sign of a healthy recovery." Should the nation be in a recession, they may announce, "More gloomy economic news tonight—economists said today that the nation's output of goods and services grew at a sluggish annual rate of less than two percent." In any event, the implication is the same—growth is unquestionably good.

Wolf Blitzer wouldn't dream of coming on the air and saying, "We've got some good news tonight—the Democrats are surging ahead of the Republicans in the polls." That would be "partisan," "taking sides," "not objective." But increased wealth is such a given that it's assumed that no other side exists—that any objective viewer would agree, and only a crank would think otherwise. It is a safe assumption, actually. If the world's politicians were all locked in a single room and told to agree on one statement, the only sentence they would be able to write is this: "Our task is to promote economic growth." In this country, Democrats and Republicans differ only over how to go about it. In the 2004 election, President Bush insisted his tax cuts for the wealthy would spur output, while John Kerry insisted the resulting deficits would hamper the economy. Back when there were still Communists, they adopted precisely the same measure of success—their effectiveness was measured in units of steel produced and grain harvested, and their five-year plans pointed forever in the same direction.

We have raised More on a pedestal; it is every bit as unchallenged an orthodoxy as the piety of Job's friends or the mechanical earth-centered universe of Ptolemy. The castle is just as imposing, surrounded by scores of think tanks and thousands of university departments. From its ramparts fly billions of dollars worth of advertising banners; its message surges through every modem. Turn on a TV and try to identify the recurring motifs. One of the most common is that increased growth benefits the world, the society, the individual. The only thing that television believes as strongly is that sunny weather is "good weather"—the meteorologists are forever apologizing if there's rain in the forecast, just as the anchorwoman furrows her brow whenever she's forced to talk about another quarter of sluggish growth. And we believe them, of course—the stock market trembles every time housing starts droop a tenth of a percent, spooking the huge mass of investors.

There is no question that growth seems desirable to us—it seems obviously, intuitively right. More is better. It fits with our understanding of the world—more means easier, more comfortable, more secure.

Whether or not this was true in the past, however, there is now a new fact in the world—a fact as threatening as Job's innocence or Copernicus's observations. A fact that threatens to render our current paradigm just as unworkable as that of Eliphaz or Ptolemy. It is, of course, the realization that the natural environment places finite limits on our behavior. That the "more" of human desire is running into physical walls it may not be able to escape. That if we press ahead in our current paths at our current pace we threaten everything else in creation, and with it ourselves. The intuitive "logic" of growth, in other words, has begun to run into counterexamples, just as the theological orthodoxy of Job's day imploded on contact with his story. The bottom line is this: If we continue to make our economics and our populations ever larger, if we continue to consume ever more of the world's natural resources, we may find ourselves and our planet deeply impoverished. The "obviousness" of growth, environmentalists are starting to realize, is obvious only if you ignore the fundamental biological and chemical facts of creation.

Ignoring these facts—insisting on ever more people living at an ever higher level—is tantamount to what I would call a "decreation" of the natural order we found on this earth. To understand the momentum of this decreation, consider a short chemistry lesson. The most powerful engine of destruction—the most extraordinary new fact—is the ever more obvious change in global climate.

Perhaps some of you have your own lawnmowers and go to the service station to fill the gas can. You will know, then, that a gallon of gasoline weighs about eight pounds. When you burn that gallon of gasoline in your power mower, or in your car, it produces about five and a half pounds of carbon in the form of carbon dioxide. The average American car driven the average American distance—about ten thousand miles—produces its own weight in carbon annually. Similarly any combustion of coal or natural gas or other fossil fuel also produces carbon dioxide—carbon with two oxygen atoms. Now, this carbon dioxide is not so dangerous to any of us as individuals—it is not like carbon monoxide, or carbon with one oxygen atom, which kills you if you inhale too much. Carbon dioxide does nothing like that—the level of CO_2 in any room is much higher than it will ever get out-doors, and it's not affecting any of us. In fact, for a very long time scientists described an engine as "clean" if it burned coal or gas or oil and produced only CO_2 and water vapor. There is only one hitch in this happy story. Carbon dioxide, by virtue of its molec-ular structure, is capable of trapping heat in the atmosphere that would otherwise radiate back out to space.

Scientists have known this for a long time—a great Swedish chemist, Svante Arrhenius, made predictions more than a century ago that are astonishingly close to the latest computer models. But no one paid much attention—most scientists, being human, assumed that the earth would take care of the extra gas we were creating with all our factories and automobiles. To be specific, they assumed that the oceans could soak up all our excess carbon dioxide. Then, in the late 1950s, a pair of California scientists per-formed a few simple experiments and showed that this was not in fact the case—that the oceans were at equilibrium for CO_2. These two scientists speculated that the excess carbon must be piling up in the atmosphere. They sent a graduate student off to Mauna Loa volcano in Hawaii to set up an instrument and find out. This machine almost immediately began to provide data showing that the level of carbon dioxide in the air was artificially high and increasing each year. It is currently 380 parts per million, and by mid-century—which is to say within the lifetime of many of the people reading these words—it will have doubled its concentration from the days before the Industrial Revolution.

There is no question that this carbon dioxide will trap heat. Mars is bitter cold because it has no CO_2; Venus is a toasty eight hundred degrees because it has an immense amount. We are happily in between, though tending in the Venusian direction. The question has been, for the last thirty years, how soon any temperature increase would appear and how dramatic it would be. That is a difficult question to answer—the climate is what scientists call a very noisy system, meaning that it fluctuates quite a lot on its own, and it is difficult to unambiguously pick out the signal of climate change through the static. The first person with the guts to make a call was James Hansen, a NASA scientist, who testified before Congress in the summer of 1988 that he was ninety-nine percent certain that the greenhouse effect had kicked in. Others disagreed, saying it was too soon yet to tell. So science went to work. By 1995, the Intergovernmental Panel on climate Change, a UN body composed of the world's leading climatologists, was ready to declare that the planet was heating and humans were the cause. In the decade since, it's as if the planet itself was peer-reviewing the science. We've had 9 of the ten warmest years on record, and they've shown us just how finely balanced the world's climate system is. Everything frozen on the planet is currently melting—glaciers in rapid retreat, the Arctic ice pack thinning like an Atkins devotee. Even phenomena as much a part of our instinctive sense of the world as the progress of the seasons are rapidly changing—at my latitude in the Northeast, spring comes on average about seven days earlier than it used to. And all that is with a relatively modest increase of about a degree Fahrenheit in global average temperature.

And the debate about whether or not global warming has started is actually much stronger than the debate about what will happen in the future. The predictions of future warming continue to sharpen and improve. According to the UN panels on climate change, we can expect an increase of global average temperature on the order of four to five degrees Fahrenheit in the next century. Now, four to five degrees may not seem so much, but in all likelihood this will be the most powerful of all the many engines driving the decreation of this planet. This climate change will happen thirty to sixty times faster than it has happened before and will leave us in a world much hotter than ever before in human history. And the effect will be devastating. Just to give you a brief idea of the effects, let's leave Job for a moment and take up the biblical story at the beginning, in the first chapter of Genesis.

The first living things that were created are plants—seed-bearing plants and fruit-bearing plants, to use the wonderfully specific biology that occurs in instance after instance. "The earth brought forth vegetation, plants yielding seed according to their own kinds, and trees bearing fruit in which is their seed, each according to its kind. And God saw that it was good." What will a temperature increase of four or five degrees do to the trees and other plants? What new facts are we introducing into the world? Well, an increase of one degree moves vegetation zones about forty miles north. The trees living here, in other words, will soon want to be living two hundred miles to the north. Where I live, the trees will want to move to Canada. If that temperature increase happens slowly enough, forests can grow along their northern edge— but only about a mile per decade at the most. With an increase in temperature of the sort we are talking about, the trees will be left stranded in the wrong climatic zone. They will not die of heat directly—just as starving people usually succumb to pneumonia of flu or dysentery, they will be so severely stressed that they will die from one of the insect or fungal attacks they would normally withstand. The computer models are very grim—hundreds of thousands of square miles of temperate forest wiped out. As they die, they will liberate carbon currently fixed in their branches and in the soil, which will accelerate the greenhouse effect. But to me that seems only a secondary problem. We will be living surrounded by dying forests, daily reminded of folly. Where I live, the hemlock is one of the dominant trees; the new computer modeling indicates that by the time I am eighty or ninety, the hemlock will be confined to Canada.

What comes next in this account? "Let the waters bring forth swarms of living creatures." Well, just as we have overcut our forests, so we have overfished our seas. But that damage is as nothing compared to what may be approaching—systemic damage to the entire marine food chain. At the moment, excess ultraviolet radiation is streaming through the hole we have cut in the ozone layer. This attacks the first layer of cells it reaches, giving us skin cancer. But if you are a single-celled creature, the effect is infinitely worse. Reports from southern latitudes this winter indicate dramatic reductions in populations of krill and plankton, which ultimately feed everything else in the ocean. But even that pales next to the effects of rapid climate change. The oceans are already starting to rise and to warm, due to polar melting and the simple fact that warm water takes up more space than cold. This will not be a science-fiction type flood—the Empire State Building will not be flooded to the fortieth floor. But if the level of the oceans increases only one meter, that will be enough to wipe out half the world's coastal marshes and wetlands—which, of course, are where so many fish spawn. Imagine the East Coast without Chesapeake Bay.

And the birds, which are supposed to "fly above the earth across the firmament of the heavens?" At the moment, their numbers are dwindling because the southern range of their habitat—the equatorial rainforests—are disappearing. Matters will only get worse if the northern forests start to die for the reasons I've given above, or if the ocean levels begin to rise. The whooping crane, for instance, which we have congratulated ourselves on saving from extinction, lives on the edge of the Gulf Coast in one Texas swamp; they are imprinted to go back to the same place each year and lay their eggs, even if that land is ever soupier and less and less able to supply the food they require. Much the same phenomenon will beset the "cattle and creeping things and beasts of the earth." We have made at least a small effort in recent decades to protect the diversity of species still alive on this continent. We have set up parks and preserves and refuges. But the grizzly bear does not live in Yellowstone through some arrangement with the Wyoming tourist board. He lives there because it is the right climatic zone—the right flora and fauna to support him. If that flora and fauna were two hundred miles to the north, that's where he'd try to go—and he'd never get there because there are a couple of interstates and a hundred fenced pastures and several small cities in the way. Thomas Lovejoy of the Smithsonian has estimated that a rapid global warming could kill off more species than the worst ice ages.

So you begin to see what I mean by this invented word "decreation." Forget for the moment the devastating effects on human beings—the toll on agriculture, the costs of protecting ports and infrastructure, the fate of Bengali peasants already stressed to the breaking point. Consider just the Genesis account. The work of the first days nullified—not entirely, since we haven't found a way to affect the alternation of day and night. But the daylight will shine on a world stripped of much of its glory. And it's not simply the greenhouse effect, of course—there are a thousand other environmental problems that we face: deforestation, the loss of farm and forest and swamp land to development, the erosion of soil. But global warming is the great example because it is so all-encompassing. We've always altered nature, of course. As a species we have come into this world not fast enough, not strong enough, not hairy enough—we've needed to alter our surroundings to thrive. To complain about it is as silly as cursing beavers because they cut trees and build dams. But always that alteration has ended at the edge of our settlements and our fields, and beyond them life has gone on largely as before. No more. Now we are able to affect the largest single physical system on the planet, the very climate. And that affects everything else. Not one inch of the planet's surface is immune to the effects of shifting temperatures. Recent estimates said that the world's coral reefs were dying at a rate of five percent annually, apparently because of bleaching from increased ocean temperatures related to the greenhouse effect. You don't need to be a mathematician to figure out that at five percent a year it won't be long before that ecosystem is all but gone—one of the most beautiful, complete, harmonious, magic environments we know. Many of you may have snorkeled off some tropical beach—hung still in the water while clouds of colored fish, moving as if one animal, swung slowly by. Let that world stand as one symbol of all we are losing.

This wholesale alteration seems so impossible—we are so used to thinking of the earth as an enormous place and human beings as small creatures. But celebrating the glory of God means constantly striving to appreciate the exact nature of his creation. The earth is a museum of divine intent, and as the museumgoers we should be responsive not just to the beautiful mosaic but also to the specifications. For example, the planet we live on is not so large after all. That is, viewed horizontally it goes on for a very long way. Not as long as it once did—the age of jet aircraft has let us girdle the globe in a day or two. Still, it's enormous—those of us who have spent time at sea know the feeling of staring off at the horizon in every direction, cutting one lonely furrow across a vast field. Vertically, however, the world is not nearly so large. Just a few miles above us—a couple of hours walk if we could walk straight up—you come to the end of the useful atmosphere. The top of Mt. Everest is about as far as you can go and still have a chance at breathing; even there, you are losing brain cells unless you get artificial oxygen. Into this narrow envelope between ground and atmospheric ceiling is squeezed pretty much everything that maintains life. It is a comparatively small reservoir, and we are busily filling it up. Since the end of World War II, by some estimates, human beings have used more natural resources than in all previous human history—that is a statistic to recall when thinking about growth.

For a while environmentalists were afraid that this small world would run out of resources. When people first talked about living in an age of limits, they meant that we would soon find ourselves without enough copper or bauxite or, most commonly, oil. In a way, it would have been beneficial if those forecasts had proved correct—we would have made the switch much sooner to more benign ways of living. But those projections underestimated the power of economics. As the cost of commodities like oil rose, so did exploration, and we found more and more—the Saudis, for instance, now estimate that they can keep current production levels for more than a century. We have coal enough to keep us going to centuries beyond that. We have come to understand that the limits, instead of being on sources, are on what scientists call "sinks." Simply put, we do not have enough places to put the waste products from our consumption of resources. Some of this problem is terrestrial—we have a harder time finding places to dump our garbage. But this largely aesthetic problem is dwarfed by our rush to fill the atmosphere with the emissions from our growth and expansion. The sky is not falling; the sky is filling up, changing its composition. As we only have one sky, this is a serious problem.

To me, this environmental devastation stands as the single great crisis of our time, surpassing and encompassing all others. It is preeminent because it must be solved now, today, in this generation. Human hatred and division and strife and poverty must be solved now, too—terrorism is just one sign of this low-grade fever. But if they are not—and human beings have been slow to solve them over the centuries—they will be around for the next generation to solve. Job is timeless—fresh when it was written, fresh now, fresh in a millennium. But the environmental crisis is not an historic and eternal crisis. It is new, and it is a timed exam—a hundred years from now, our descendants will not be trying to solve the greenhouse effect. We will solve it, or it will be too late to solve, and endurance will be the challenge. When I say that the environmental crisis is not an historic crisis, I mean that even in its broadest terms it has come upon us suddenly. Not until Rachel Carson wrote *Silent Spring* in the early 1960s did we consider the chemical legacy we were leaving the planet. Not until a British satellite noticed a hole in the Antarctic ozone in 1984 did we imagine that we might be altering the rays of the sun. It may not have been until 2003, when a heat wave killed twenty thousand western Europeans in a fortnight, that most of the developed world really got serious about climate; and even now we in the U.S. have barely noticed. And if we are to solve these problems, we must do so in the next few decades—the daunting mathematics of exponential growth means that our enormous numbers and vast industrial societies must somehow be reined in quickly or else double and then double again—and then what? Nothing good.

The clear messages we see around us—the increased temperatures, the sickening die-off of species that may be as high as ten a day (ten chains of being stretching back to creation), the eroding ozone—these messages all tell us that we are badly out of balance. That we, the products of creation's later days, are destroying our elders. That having been given, in the words of Deuteronomy, a land of flowing streams, with springs and underground waters welling up in valleys and hills, a land of wheat and barley, of vines and fig trees and pomegranates, a land of olive trees and honey, a land where you may eat bread without scarcity, where you will lack nothing—that having been given this land we are failing. We live in an age of metaphor become reality. When God says, through Jeremiah, "I brought you into a plentiful land to enjoy its fruits and good things. But when you came in you defiled my land, and made my heritage an abomination," it was not at the time an environmental comment—the Israelites were not being scolded for deforesting the Mediterranean but instead for a variety of vices and carelessness, a moral pollution. We still practice many of those vices and are as morally careless, but we now pollute God's pleasant vision in a physical sense as well. We *are* defiling the land. And we can see metaphoric vision as possible reality as well. If you have spent a good deal of time studying the greenhouse effect, it is not comfortable to read the warning in the twenty-fourth chapter of Isaiah: "Behold, the Lord will lay waste the earth and make it desolate, and he will twist its surface and scatter its inhabitants. . . . The earth mourns and withers, the world languishes and withers; the heavens languish together with the earth. . . . Therefore the inhabitants of the earth are scorched. . . . All joy has reached its eventide; the gladness of the earth is banished." This is not a farfetched vision. It is a reasonably accurate description of what we are accomplishing in the space of a few short decades. It is the physical fact that we now must factor into every idea, every ideology, every plan for our future.

* * *

So far we have considered how this current orthodoxy of More stands up to the outside world. But there is also another fact that counters the standard assumptions about material growth and physical acquisition. It is more nebulous than the physical fact—there are no instruments that can accurately detect and measure it—but it is in many ways just as important. And that fact is this: the amazing expansion of material possessions and consumer convenience may not actually be making us as happy as the advertisers and economists say. Our current ideals may be as incompatible with our inner world as with our outer one.

I call it a fact, but it is, of course, debatable. Endlessly debatable, for what would pass for hard evidence? There are Gallup surveys of personal happiness, which show that it peaked among Americans in the mid–1950s, but it seems a pretty big question to leave up to the pollsters. Each of us must look around and decide—is our culture as satisfying, as fulfilling, as we want it to be? Are our neighbors deeply and truly happy? Is the American suburb, the zenith of every material ideal, a profoundly nourishing place? If the answer is no, then we have a deeply disturbing fact, one that should shake our moral and economic universes as thoroughly as the greenhouse effect shakes our physical world.

The notion that money does not buy happiness is, of course, hardly new. But it has always been the oppositionists, the people who don't fit into their societies, who have expressed it. Jesus did, for one, though his answer to the sorrowful rich man is not an important part of our modern Christian culture. Since then, it has been mostly saints and cranks who have upheld this view, and while we may pay homage to Francis or to Thoreau, we are likely to act as if we really think they are nutty exceptions to a general rule.

I think, however, that this assurance is becoming harder to sustain, and for an interesting reason. Always in times past, there seemed to be a great deal more material progress to anticipate; if we were not yet happy it was because we still needed to move a little further along the transition from brute labor to machines, from the threat of scarcity to the certainty of abundance, from too little to plenty. By any reasonable definition, we who live in the well-off sections of the Western world have now accomplished that transition. Within our lifetimes—within the same lifetimes that saw the fact of global environmental damage suddenly arise—we have reached some new point of material saturation. From this new vantage point, things feel very different. It is increasingly difficult to convince ourselves that somehow more will mean better.

I began to realize this while watching television. And I do mean watching television. Almost a decade ago I wrote a book—*The Age of Missing Information*—for which I performed an unusual experiment. I found the largest cable TV system in

America; it's in Fairfax, Virginia, and provides viewers with roughly one hundred channels. For one day in the spring of 1990 I arranged to have each of those hundred channels videotaped, leaving me with a pile of about two thousand hours of videotape that I spent the next year watching. This cable system had six shopping channels. It had five religious channels. Two sports channels. A local weather station and a national weather station. It had a channel that simply broadcast, twenty-four hours a day, the arrival and departure screens from the Dulles and National airports in Washington, D.C. It even had a channel that was split into four screens, so that you could watch the three networks and PBS simultaneously. As I sat there and watched, it became clear to me that we must live in a society where for most people the very idea of "need" has been banished. What other kind of culture could offer a mass market for, say, a coat hanger that won't "rust and dirty your clothes"? Already owning something is no reason not to buy it again—the Regina Housekeeper "makes an excellent second vacuum, maybe to put upstairs," and "some Armani would make a nice gift even if it isn't his *main* fragrance." All day long a particularly annoying ad for Pearle Vision Centers kept insisting that you needed two pairs of glasses so that your frames could match your mood. Buy so that you'll have room to buy more—Rubbermaid produces the commercial that really sums up this phenomenon. "From the day I was born," a lady is saying, "I collected so much stuff!" (The picture shows a sad family impossibly hemmed in by their possessions.) "So we stowed our stuff in stuff from Rubbermaid." (The house is now shown bare, save for big plastic boxes full of gear.) "Then we were so unstuffed—Hey! We need more stuff!" (Family charges happily out the door, waving hands in the air.) The best ad of all, and the one that was on the most frequently by my rough count, was for a new liquid called Jet-Dri that you add to your dishwasher during the rinse cycle. Why? Because "you can't always see it, but it's there. *Residue* from foods, detergent, minerals, clinging to everything your dishwasher washed." That is to say, your expensive appliance, which carefully sloshes soapy hot water and then clean hot water over your dishes, actually doesn't work. It leaves behind a *residue*. You can't see this residue—it's *invisible*. The result of "detergent," or "minerals," or "food." Minerals? Aren't we supposed to have more of them in our diets? Food particles? How could invisible food particles hurt you? When they were visible, you were eating them. Forget about trying to serve God and money—we have to try to serve God and our dishwashers and Rubbermaid and the J.C. Penney Shopping Channel and the man who wants to sell you his Raise Your Kids cassette course.

That's the old news. But the new news that came jumping out of the screen at me, and to which I've already alluded, is this: Things aren't progressing. I don't mean that we're not getting richer (though we're not—between 1969 and the present, median family income in real dollars has not risen at all). I mean that even if we all made twice as much money, our cash could buy us very little additional ease or even luxury. Daily life *has scarcely changed* between 1960, when I was born, and the present; it is hard to see how it is going to change much in the future, at least in attractive ways. We've gone about as far as we can go.

Earlier in the century, people learned to talk across long distances on telephones, to travel easily and routinely. School became standard, even in remote areas. The occupations divided and specialized, replacing self-sufficient ways of life. Appliances transformed the home. Birth control allowed limits on reproduction. Easy refrigeration changed the way we thought about food. Most people's bathrooms moved indoors. People washed their bodies daily, not weekly. Medicine eliminated most childhood deaths and made all lives healthier and more secure. Radio and then television spread a universal culture. Farming mechanized to the point where most people were freed from the soil. All of these changes affected daily life enormously, and all of them took place before 1960. We even had computers when I was born, though they were huge and not so powerful. Certainly the Internet has turned them into different creatures and helped refashion the texture of our daily lives—still, it's mostly been a matter of trading one screen for another. Every study shows that the amount of leisure time continues to shrink, and the number of work hours continues to grow. We're not being freed from labor, or even paperwork—the print button is the most popular stop on most keyboards.

The real proof is that you can watch TV shows that are thirty years old without them seeming weird. All the changes have been social—the women's movement, for instance—and not material. Physically, life on a contemporary sitcom is a lot like life in Harriet and Ozzie's house. If you walked into Samantha's kitchen in "Bewitched," you would know how to make breakfast. In fact, you'd use many of the same products—in almost every category, the dominant brands in the 1960s (Hershey's cocoa, Wonder bread) remain the dominant brands today. If you walked into Tabitha's playroom, as I wrote in the book, you'd recognize most of the toys—Barbie for sure. (The ideal of feminine beauty has not appreciably shifted—Barbie's measurements remain standard.) Even the clothes in the closet would be more or less familiar—a contemporary Samantha might have tossed out the various miracle synthetics in favor of cotton, but that's it. Her social life might well have changed, too—she'd probably have a career, and on her way to work she might have to step over homeless people. But the world of material artifacts would be remarkably static.

What a contrast this presents with earlier decades. The average American home of 1940 was radically different from the average American home of 1910, say. It's that time of rapid progress we're really thinking about when we tell ourselves stories about the dynamic twentieth-century. This fact of our current stasis runs so contrary to our prevailing myth, however, that it's very hard for us to accept, or even see. We tell ourselves that we must be on the brink of some set of new developments that will revolutionize our lives the way the car or record player or television revolutionized the lives of our predecessors. The trouble with this pervasive line of thinking is that there isn't much left to streamline. How are we going to get around more conveniently than we do in our fleets of cars? Elroy, on "The Jetsons," prepared dinner by pushing a button in the wall. Is that much different from slapping a prepared entree into a microwave? Even if we invent a super microwave that cuts microwaving time in half, does the transition from two minutes to one minute amount to any real progress? You can hook the microwave to a superconducting electric line; you can manufacture the entree with genetic manipulation of cows and corn—it may be slightly more efficient, but in terms of day-to-day living, it won't be much different. Your new PDA can call home and surf the web and take a picture, but when you get right down to it, so what? And anyway, who wants one?

Who wants one? This is a remarkable threat to the orthodoxy of the day. If we ever started to ask that question in large numbers the world would necessarily change. "Have you noticed that it doesn't make you happy?" That is as explosive a question as the one Job asks his friends—"Haven't you seen that bad men live out long and pleasant lives and their cows don't miscarry?" It is an old fact brought out into the open—a threatening notion that does not fit with our prevailing ideology. And, as I have said, it is not the only such fact.

Every period in history fancies itself unique and pivotal, and especially in the shadow of the approaching millennium it is probably best to downplay such talk. But it fascinates me that we live at a moment of confluence. For a very long time the artists and sages and saints (and kooks) have maintained that nonattachment and simplicity and the flight from materialism are necessary for the good life; now, as I have pointed out, their message stands to spread more widely simply because the gospel of happiness through material progress grows less persuasive the richer we become. And at the same precise moment in history, the saints and sages are joined by the atmospheric chemists and the computer modelers who are asking precisely the same kinds of questions about growth. Is it desirable? Is it possible?

The orthodox economic theory has an answer to all these questions, of course. The easiest answer to our environmental dilemma, the one preferred by politicians, is that we need new technology. That the basic momentum of our civilization can be maintained, if only we have better pollution control equipment. The Eliphazes of the moment insist that there is no need to worry—"hydrogen cars," they keep whispering. This is not the *wrong* answer. It will be immensely helpful if we have more efficient appliances and cars that get better gas mileage or run on electricity. Some of these changes are coming, and they could come faster if we had better leadership. Consider just one example: in the 1970s, we had a tax credit for solar energy, and in 1983 there were thirty thousand Americans employed in the solar energy field. Ronald Reagan repealed that tax credit, and within a year only two thousand workers remained in the field. But I do not believe that technological changes alone will be enough—the math simply does not add up. Without basic changes in the ways we live our lives, I think we will make scant progress. One more short chemistry lesson may help explain why.

Consider the greenhouse effect once more as an example. The main culprit is the gas carbon dioxide, which unlike carbon monoxide or nitrous oxide or low-level ozone has no damaging direct effect on human beings. There is something else unique about CO_2 as well, and that is that there is no way to remove it from fossil fuel combustion. You can fix a car's engine so that it emits next to no carbon monoxide or particulates; you can filter the emissions from a coal-burning power plant so that almost no sulfur or nitrogen comes out of the stack. But there is nothing you can do to cut down on the amount of carbon dioxide an engine or boiler produces—it is an inevitable by-product of fossil fuel combustion. And to stabilize the global climate at current levels of disruption—to hold the temperature at its current historically elevated level—the United Nations estimated in 2001 that we would need an immediate sixty percent reduction in fossil fuel use. Anything approaching that figure simply cannot happen from conversion to alternative energy sources—they won't be available in time, or in sufficient quantity, even to offset the increased usage of energy among developing nations. Consider hydrogen cars. They sound like a good idea, and indeed President Bush has made them the cornerstone of what passes for his energy policy. But their stock, literally, has been decimated as new technical obstacles keep cropping up; realistic forecasters estimate they'll account for five percent of the market at best by 2030. Which means there will be far more gasoline powered cars on the road in three decades then there are now—here, but especially in China and India, which are just learning the joys of being behind the wheel.

The late Donella Meadows and her colleagues have recently produced a third update of the computer simulations that undergirded their "Limits to Growth" report in the early 1970s. They show that unless we quickly change the exponential growth rate in consumption we may soon overshoot the carrying capacity of this planet . . . and watch our societies collapse—not to mention the effect that it will have on every other species. Such a translation to sustainability would not be easy, of course. If there is one thing that every politician on earth agrees about, it's that economic growth is the raison d'être of our civilization. And you can understand why when you watch what happened in recent American history. George H. W. Bush's recession—eighteen months of the largest economy in the history of the world growing no larger—produced real misery and want. But the lesson is not that we need to do everything we can think of, including weakening our environmental laws, to start growing fast again. The lesson is that we need to quickly figure out ways to guarantee decent lives for everyone without needing constant expansion. Because further expansion is not physically, ecologically, desirable. We are getting signals from the world around us—signals about increasing temperatures, drastically increasing extinctions, reduced levels of ozone. These are signals about the proper size of our civilization and its economies. If we do not heed them, we will pay. Our world will be ecologically impoverished, and as I have been trying to say, it will be spiritually impoverished as well.

These signals would be recognizable to Job, or to Copernicus, or to anyone else who has lived at a moment when inconvenient facts emerged to upset tired truth. They are stressful moments, of course—we do not enjoy the blessing of living in uninteresting times. But they are passages filled with opportunity as well as risk. We need a new vision that accommodates the new facts—a vision, like Job's or Copernicus's, that sees a little further toward the beautiful and ineffable heart of our existence.

Perhaps the conclusions I come to will seem unrealistic or radical to you, but I hope not. "Unrealistic" and "radical" are two of the words often used to discredit environmentalists who try to move beyond the most obvious and easy applications of common sense. When people say "unrealistic," they mean that they're quite willing to recycle their cans and bottles. Which is a very good thing—I'm all for recycling. But at best recycling is a sort of calisthenics for the marathon that faces us; as a solution to the deepest crises that we face, *it* is the fantasy. As for "radical," that word has never bothered me that much. I grew up in Lexington, Massachusetts, the birthplace of American liberty, and I made my summer money giving tours of the Battle Green, dressed in a tricorne hat and talking about those brave radicals who resisted the status quo. In any event, it seems to me that in the case of the environment the best definition of radical, if by that you insist on meaning extreme and unbalanced, consists of continuing to behave as we are behaving. It is deeply radical to say, we have five billion people on this planet; let's have ten billion and see what happens. It is extremely radical to say, let's keep driving till we change the chemistry of the atmosphere and see what happens. It is tragically radical to contemplate the fact that when you were born you shared the planet with perhaps thirty million other species, and when you die there may be one-tenth that number. I'm tired of this radicalism, and fearful of its results. Past the physically and emotionally spent orthodoxy of the moment, I sense, if even vaguely, a deeper reality that is beckoning us joyfully onward.

CHAPTER

2

Job, I have contended, was struggling with the orthodoxy of his day—with the "obvious" notion that God dispensed prosperity to the good and punishment to the wicked. And we—late 21st-century Westerners—are beginning to struggle with an orthodoxy of our own—the central economic and social idea that more is better, that growth is necessary. These two orthodoxies, I have tried to show, are similar in that an examination of the facts (Job's innocence, our environmental predicament) call them into serious question.

But they are similar in another way as well, a deeper and more organic connection. Both stem from the assumption that human beings are and should be at the center of everything. They are outgrowths of the human-centered or anthropocentric understanding that has dominated modern human culture. Job's friends believed that God's calculus was their own, that he made his plans with regard to our very human ideas of justice and fair play. We believe at some intuitive level that it is all right to use everything that surrounds us for our own benefit—that creation matters because it is of use to us. This understanding—this bias—is the underlying orthodoxy from which these and other beliefs stem, the buried root that sends up runners throughout the garden.

Lynn White Jr., in a massively influential 1967 article in *Science* magazine, traced this notion to the beginning of the Bible, to the Genesis notion of humans holding dominion over the earth, and surely Job's friends were governed consciously or not by the companion idea that we are made in God's image. There's no question that White is largely right in his claim that this biblical sanction has been a major driving force behind our hubris. As Aldo Leopold, the wisest of all twentieth-century ecologists, said, "Abraham knew what the land was for—the land was to drip milk and honey into Abraham's mouth." Wallace Stegner, that marvelous chronicler of the West, once wrote: "Our sanction to be a weed species living at the expense of every other species and of Earth itself can be found in the injunction God gave to the newly created Adam and Eve in Genesis." In New York State, where I live, the best state legislator on environmental issues was speaking to a church group recently, and he said that he was an environmentalist *in spite* of being a sincere Christian. There are many, many people estranged from the Judeo-Christian tradition, people who have taken up New Age practices or left spirituality behind altogether, because they think that right from the start the Bible is incompatible with their hopes for a sustainable planet not entirely dominated by human beings.

Long and learned debates have taken place about the meaning of the Genesis passages, of course, and I have little to add to them here—the consensus, as I understand it, is that at the very least most interpreters agree that God, who after all had gone to the trouble of creating myriad species and who had called them "good," did not understand dominion to include thoughtless destruction for short-term gain. Be that as it may, the anthropocentric concept is embedded in many non-Christian human societies as well. The idea that everything revolves around us seems to be an "obvious" feature of advanced cultures.

I am more interested in the reply that God provides to this obviousness when he speaks from the whirlwind at the end of the book of Job. It is, I think, a shatteringly radical answer, one that undercuts every bit of the orthodoxies that entwine us. As

Gutierrez writes, "God speaks, but in an unpredictable way—making no reference to concrete problems and therefore not responding to the distress and questions of Job. This does not seem correct. What God says is disconcerting to the reader, but Job seems to understand it. Our aim is to share this understanding."

The first disconcerting aspect of the long speech from the whirlwind is its tone. This is a deeply sarcastic God speaking, one who finds it no longer possible to contain himself in the face of the deep and assured misunderstandings of Job and his friends.

> Who is this whose ignorant words
> > smear my design with darkness?
> Stand up now like a man;
> > I will question you: please, instruct me.

Job, wisely, refrains from making any answer as God begins a tour of his universe, never dropping his caustic tone.

> Where were you when I planned the earth?
> > Tell me, if you are so wise.
> Do you know who took its dimensions,
> > measuring its length with a cord?
> What were its pillars built on?
> > Who laid down its cornerstone. . . [?]

The catalogue continues, as God badgers Job about whether he stopped the waters of the oceans at the beaches or set the sun to rising or knows where the snow is stored. The speech is notable for many things, not least among them the ferocity and beauty of the language ("Have you ever commanded morning / or guided dawn to its place— / to hold the corners of the sky / and shake off the last few stars? / All things are touched with color; / the whole world is changed").

Even more notable, however, is the setting. God is describing a world without people—a world that existed long before people, and that seems to have its own independent meaning. Most of the action takes place long before the appearance of humans, and on a scale so powerful and vast that we are small indeed in the picture of things. Almost the only reference to our species in this species-filled speech makes the point absolutely clear:

> Who cuts a path for the thunderstorm
>   and carves a road for the rain—
> to water the desolate wasteland,
>   the land where no man lives;
> to make the wilderness blossom
>   and cover the desert with grass?

God seems untroubled by the notion of a place where no man lives—in fact, God says he makes it rain there even though it has no human benefit at all. God makes the *wilderness blossom*—what stronger way could there be to make the point, what more overpowering fact to rebut the notion that we are forever at the center of all affairs. The first meaning, I think, of God's speech to Job is that we are a part of the whole order of creation—simply a part.

And that is of course a radical idea—far more subversive than Marxism or Leninism or Maoism or any of the other seditions we've grown up fearing. Those radicalisms are of course deeply human-centered; the radical voice from the whirlwind seems to assign us a less exalted role. To be a part of creation instead of its center is as mind-boggling as the Copernican understanding that we were revolving around a center instead of serving as one. It undercuts every one of our orthodoxies.

And yet it should not come as a complete surprise. It is certainly not the first such hint in Scripture, which begins with God's creation of everything else, and God's instructions to the living creatures to be fruitful and multiply and fill the earth. What was Noah, after all, but the original radical conservationist, assigned to save a breeding pair of everything from the snail darter to the passenger pigeon to the grizzly bear? What was the ark but the prototype wildlife refuge, containing species in the hope they would one day again spread out around the world in their natural habitats?

My favorite vision of this balanced world comes from the familiar 104th Psalm, which of course begins with creation, using almost the same images as the voice from the whirlwind but a kinder, gentler tone. God sets the earth on its foundations and covers it "with the deep as with a garment" so that the waters stood above the mountains until God rebukes them and they flee; then he sets "a bound which they should not pass." The psalm goes on to describe the springs gushing in the valleys, watering the beasts of the field and also the wild asses and the birds of the air. "Thou dost cause the grass to grow for the cattle, and plants for man to cultivate, that he may bring forth food from the earth, and wine to gladden the heart of man, oil to make his face shine, and bread to strengthen man's heart." So our needs are to be met, and met handsomely by the world—not just bread, but oil so our faces shine; not just food, but wine so our hearts are glad. But that is only part of the story. "The trees of the Lord are [also] watered abundantly, the cedars of Lebanon which he planted. In them the birds build their nests; the stork has her home in the fir trees. The high mountains are *for* the wild goats; the rocks are a refuge *for* the badgers." Not "the wild goats live in the high mountains." The high mountains are for the wild goats. Not "the badgers seek refuge in the rocks." The rocks are a refuge for the badgers. "Thou makest darkness, and it is night, when all the beasts of the forest creep forth. The young lions roar for their prey, seeking their food from God." "In wisdom," says the psalmist, "thou has made them all; the earth is full of thy creatures. Yonder is the sea, great and wide, which teems with things innumerable, living things both small and great. There go the ships, and Leviathan which thou didst form to sport in it." Didst form to sport in it—anyone who has seen a humpback whale breeching understands that phrase, and the world of meaning it conveys. Those who make fun of the "save the whales" crowd make fun of God—they substitute their judgment as to what's important for his.

That clear evidence has always undercut our anthropocentric bias, at least to those few who would honestly examine it. It is as plain in its way as the travelers' stories that Job refers to of the prospering wicked. And if most have turned their backs on the evidence, there have always been a few who saw more clearly. Take for instance the great American naturalist John Muir. Muir was actually born in Scotland, but at a young age moved to a homestead in the Midwest. His father was a devoted Christian, not to mention a child abuser—he used his belt to force young Muir to memorize the entire New Testament and most of the Old by the time he was ten. Not surprisingly, young John left home as soon as he was able, and before long set out on a marvelous adventure, a thousand-mile hike from Indiana to the Gulf Coast of Florida through what was still largely wilderness. He kept a journal as he walked, and in that journal the categories of his orthodox upbringing are clashing with the facts around him. He takes months to pick his way painfully through the swamps of Florida, for instance, with briars tangling him at every turn, and mosquitoes mounting their nighttime assaults. At night, writing in his journal, he remembers the insistence of his old preacher that the world was made "especially for man." Indulging in a little sarcasm of his own, he pokes fun at those who believe that in the divine plan "whales are storehouses of oil for us, in lighting our dark ways until the discovery of the Pennsylvania oil wells," and that God planted the first hemp plant so that someday we might be able to wrap packages and "hang the wicked." The utilitarian interpretation, he insists, is simply not supported by the evidence of his eyes or his thorn-scratched body. But he does not rest with this rather obvious point—he goes on, in the words of Wisconsin theologian J. Baird Callicott, to "expound an alternative environmental theology" in language that still rings today. "It never seems to occur to these far-seeing teachers that Nature's object in making animals and plants might possibly be first of all the happiness of each one of them, not the creation of all for the happiness of one. Why should man value himself as more than a small part of the one great unit of creation? And what creature of all that the Lord has taken the pains to make is not essential to the completeness of the unit—the cosmos? The universe would be incomplete without man; but it would also be incomplete without the smallest transmicroscopic creature that dwells beyond our conceitful eyes and knowledge." He goes on to appropriate the language of the second chapter of Genesis: "From the dust of the earth, from the common elementary fund, the Creator has made Homo sapiens. From the same material he has made every other creature, however noxious and insignificant to us. They are earth-born companions and fellow mortals. . . . Doubtless these creatures are happy and fill the place assigned them by the great Creator of us all. . . . How narrow we selfish, conceited creatures are in our sympathies! How blind to the rights of all the rest of creation! With what dismal irreverence do we speak of our fellow mortals! They are part of God's family, unfallen, undepraved and cared for with the same species of tenderness and love as is bestowed on angels in heaven and saints on earth."

Muir was writing decades before the word "ecology" was even in use, and yet he intuitively understood that life on this planet was a fabric, not a collection of individual threads. Many of us live in the cities or suburbs, and so the evidence of this complex whole is less obvious to us—these environments *are* designed with human beings at the very center, manicured to remove the thorns and sloped to drain the swamps. But we do have access still to a great deal of secondhand information, on television and in books, which should serve to remind us of the world around us. Not just the furry and cute animals, but the whole that they compose, a complex and gorgeous artifact of the mind of God that we insist on stripping down, simplifying, weakening, impoverishing. Every day we learn more about this world. Two decades ago the word "rain forest" was hardly a part of our active vocabularies; now most of us have begun to realize what a perfect example of this huge fabric it represents. When we burn down a tropical rain forest, we of course destroy the unique species that depend on that habitat—by some estimates ten species disappear daily, taking not only their own irreplaceable *beingness*, but also whatever utilitarian use, say as medicines, they might have for us. The smoke from those burnings adds immense clouds of carbon dioxide to the atmosphere—perhaps fifteen percent of the total of manmade CO_2. Deforestation also removes an amazing sink for carbon dioxide: we think of the tropical jungles as lush, and they are, but the biomass is in the air—in the triple and quadruple canopies with their enormous leaves, in the vines that link them. The soil is actually quite poor, and once the land has been cut, you get grass at best, and even that for only a few years—never again the mighty trees that soak up the CO_2. On the grass you pasture cattle—cattle are able to convert grass to food because they have anaerobic bacteria in their intestines that digest cellulose. As they digest, those bacteria give off methane (anyone who has lived on a farm can testify that cows are reliable sources of methane) and methane, it turns out, is an even more potent greenhouse gas than CO_2—molecule for molecule it traps twenty times as much heat.

The level of methane in the atmosphere has more than tripled in the last couple of centuries, to the point where it is far higher now than ever in the earth's history. And cows are not the only source. As we clear rainforests, we leave immense piles of dead wood lying around. Termites can eat this wood because they have the same bacteria in their guts. How much trouble can little termites cause? Because of the fantastic destruction of the earth's forests— a destruction fueled in no small part by the demand for wood and beef in the rich world—there are now between one-half and three-fourths of a ton of termites for every man, woman, and child on the face of the planet.

The facts—the testimony of the psalmist, the evidence of our own eyes and ears, the emerging understanding of the atmospheric chemists—lead to the same conclusions that God draws for Job in his mighty speech. Our anthropocentric bias is swept away. The question becomes this: what will replace it?

*   *   *

Humility, first and foremost. That is certainly Job's reaction. If we are not, as we currently believe, at the absolute epicenter of the created world, then we need to learn to humble ourselves. Humility is usually regarded as a spiritual attribute, a state of mind. But I want to focus for a short while on its more practical aspects—on what it might mean to walk more lightly on this earth, with more regard for the other life around us. None of what I have to say will come as any great surprise to anyone—most of the recipes for environmental improvement are widely known if little followed. Still, with God's sarcastic voice echoing in our minds, it makes sense to restate some of the obvious prescriptions.

As many have pointed out, environmental destruction is the result of an equation: population times level of consumption times efficiency of consumption equals impact. We have tended to focus on the efficiency issues—new technologies, better cars, recycling, and so on—because they are politically and emotionally the most palatable: they allow us to avoid the question of our place on the planet, they offer us the possibility of extending our current patterns of use for at least another generation or two. But as I have tried to point out, some of the specific physical characteristics of our current environmental predicaments mean that it is unlikely that by simply improving our technology we can avoid our troubles. Since carbon dioxide emissions, for instance, are an inevitable byproduct of fossil fuel consumption, and since for the foreseeable future much of our economic growth and expansion will be powered by fossil fuels, we need to ask quite seriously whether that growth is desirable, or whether there are other types of solutions we might turn to—solutions that acknowledge that our convenience and comfort is not the paramount goal of creation.

Consider one small example. America's greatest environmental sin is its complete reliance on private automobiles for transit, a reliance that grows with each passing year. By some estimates, we can expect half again as many cars on our roads within a few decades; clearly, improving mileage standards for those cars by half will only hold carbon dioxide emissions steady in place. But what if we began a large-scale attempt to shift much of our urban and suburban transit to buses, trains—and bicycles. The bicycle is in fact every bit as *technological* as an automobile, but it runs entirely on the solar energy provided by the food we eat. In some ways it is not as convenient as the car; in other ways (parking, for instance) it is more so. But the point is that learning to rely more heavily on our own muscles means forgetting the notion that we are "above" such things. That idea is dangerous spiritually and it is dangerous environmentally, in large part because we are exporting it around the globe.

Any discussion of America's role in the global environment needs to include not only the fact of our vastly disproportionate resource use and pollution production, but also the fact of our largest export: movies and television programs. That is to say, our vision of the good life, which is beamed out around the world in countless languages twenty-four hours a day, which is watched attentively in African villages and Czech cities and Colombian hill towns. As long as our vision of the good life remains in its current form, the power of those images will lead others to follow our example, with disastrous results for all of us. Consider the bicycle again: developing countries around the globe depend heavily on bicycles for individual urban transit. But under the spell of our definition of "modern," leaders of those communities have begun the rapid conversion to auto-based transit systems. Some Chinese cities have now banned bikes from their urban cores because they slow down car traffic; the Beijing auto show has become one of the city's hottest tickets. If the Chinese continue to see their economy grow by 9 percent a year, it's a safe bet they will soon be driving cars in numbers approaching ours. And India too. It all means tremendous quantities of carbon dioxide and other pollutants spilling into the atmosphere, a universally devastating development. And yet it is too much to expect that their desires for convenience, comfort, style, sexiness, and so on won't be much like ours; it is too much to expect that we will go on living our way, and they theirs. One or the other is going to change. I was in Thailand not long ago, and met with a number of Buddhist leaders, including one wonderful man who said to me, "You know, we had a pretty good thing going here for several thousand years. Our culture reproduced itself pretty well, and life went on. Once TV was introduced, it took about five years for all of that to break down." Thailand, at least in part as a result, is now an ecological disaster, its forests logged to the ground, its paddy fields, some of them thousands of years old, turned over to agribusiness, its mangrove swamps destroyed. The city of Bangkok, once the Venice of Asia, has filled in all its old canals and built roads, which are now the scene of constant, unmoving gridlock. A haze of leaded gasoline fumes chokes the city. And Thailand is just on the cutting edge of change that is taking place around the world. We have managed to create the global village that Marshall McLuhan promised. The problem is that the global village is more like a global shopping mall. The only information that is easily passed between cultures is information like "Coke is it" or "Buy a Toyota."

This discussion of humility, then, brings us squarely to the problem of global poverty. We should, long ago, have done a better job of sharing our global resources, but the forces of Christian charity and human compassion have not been strong enough to overcome our own desire for more. Now we must act from humility—from the recognition that the planet's resources (including its supply of atmosphere in which to dump our waste) are indeed limited, and that sharing them is not only right but necessary. We move here from the realm of compassion, and even of justice, to the realm of cold reality. We are one human family—like it or not. Carbon dioxide mixes freely above borders—like it or not. China owns half the world's coal reserves, and coal, as it happens, produces more CO_2 per BTU than any other source of energy. If China decides to burn that coal then it can, entirely by itself, double the CO_2 concentration in the atmosphere. And it is safe, I think, to predict that it will do so unless we in the West provide it with alternative technologies—and with alternative visions of what constitutes a decent life. If we cannot tolerate a billion Chinese living at our level of consumption, and if we cannot live at that level without their attempting to emulate us, then we had best see if we can't manage to change a little. I was in New York City in the spring of 1992 for the preparatory conferences that preceded the Rio Earth Summit, and one woman who had been representing American church groups at the talks said something to me that sounded very true: "The poor countries of the world are saying to the rich countries of the world, 'We have a right to live at the same level you do. But you can determine what that level is going to be.'" I think there is no more concise statement of our environmental future. "The poor countries of the world are saying to the rich countries of the world, 'We have a right to live at the same level you do. But you can determine what that level is going to be.'"

But consumption, of course, is only part of the equation. Another is population, and here again the proud and insistent claims of our human traditions—and our genes—will need to be limited if we are going to make progress. This has always been a difficult issue for those of us in the Jewish and Christian traditions, of course—the commandment that we are to be fruitful and multiply has been a sanction for our expansion to a globe of nearly six billion citizens, with perhaps as many again on the way. Unlike the call to dominion, the problem here is not one of misreading—humans are clearly instructed to increase their numbers until they fill the earth (just as birds and fish were instructed to do, in no less ringing terms, a few verses earlier). But it is also clear that population has become a terrible pressure—along with our ways of life in the rich world, the single most important contributor to the erosion of the world's environment. The world groans to support the people already here—look at food supply as just one example. The gains of the Green Revolution have largely been realized—food production grew at a four or five percent annual rate between the end of World War II and the middle of the 1980s. Now the environmental problems people have been warning about for decades are beginning to kick in. The erosion of topsoil, the salinization of fields due to overirrigation, the erratic weather—all have combined to hold yield growths essentially flat in recent years. Agronomists report, for instance, that aquifers are shrinking so rapidly they need to drill ever-deeper wells. As a result, the world's per capita supply of calories is no longer growing.

Happily, I don't think it needs to be such a theological problem for those of us considering the command to be fruitful and multiply. I have long maintained that the church calendar needs one additional holiday, this one a festive celebration of the one commandment we have actually managed to fulfill. We have done it—we have filled the earth. In fact, we may have overdone it, overfilled the earth to the point where our reproduction throws into question every other goal God set for us. This is one injunction we can cross off our list, and the sooner the better. Having accomplished this goal, we can set forthrightly about the task of international family planning, providing as a nation access to birth control for people everywhere. And we can practice what we preach at home as well—we are used to thinking of overpopulation as a developing world problem, but of course a child born in suburban America will produce forty times the CO_2 and other waste in a lifetime as a child born in sub-Saharan Africa. When I was touring the country to promote my first book, *The End of Nature*, people asked one question more than any other: should I use cloth or paper diapers? A good question, and hard to answer—paper diapers require cutting trees and they take up landfill space; cloth diapers on the other hand require energy to heat the water for washing. Finally I realized that the correct answer to these people was this: you should pay more attention to the question of how many babies you plan to diaper. Stabilizing a finite planet's human population is a necessary first step to restoring the balance of creation that we have knocked so disastrously out of whack.

All these issues—technology, efficiency, population—require one thing: an understanding, such as the understanding provided Job, that we do not live at the center, that we are not important out of all proportion to everything else. But day after day we are assaulted with just the opposite message, the notion that our desire is of utter and paramount importance. To say that we live in a consumer society is to say that we define ourselves by how we consume—by how we desire. And these self-definitions are relentlessly manipulated and shaped. At the same time that I was watching my thousands of hours of TV, I did another experiment: I spent twenty-four hours atop the mountain near my house, trying to see how the world would appear if nature was our main source of information about the world. As the night wore on atop the mountain, of course, I was wide awake, staring at the millions of stars that crowd the sky in our remote, unlit part of the world. "During the day," I wrote in my book, "when the sun blots out the stars and confines our sight to distances of a few miles, it's no wonder that we consider ourselves and our concerns all-important. Even the sun, the one distant object that we can see, seems to have a direct one-to-one relationship with our planet, to be there for our use. But at night this illusion ends—suddenly we can see the infinite around us. It is impossible to stand under the stars and not feel small." Switch on the tube, however, and that intuition vanishes. The idea of standing under the stars and feeling how small you are—that's not a television idea. Everything on television tells you the opposite—that you're the most important person, and that people are all that matter. "We do it all for you"; "Have it your way"; the immortal "This Bud's for you." The endless parade of jesters to entertain *you*, the obsequious newscasts that bring the story *you* want to *your* living room. It's what *you* want—"The consumer is our god," the man who picks the music for MTV told *Rolling Stone*. "Millions of dollars are spent to find out what the viewers want to see."

This ceaseless toadying and curtseying and currying of our favor—for we, after all, can provide the dollars and the ratings they desire—inevitably distorts our view of the world. What counts? People count. If Brandon Tartikoff, the former NBC programming genius, rewrote the book of Genesis, people would be created on Day One and Noah's Ark would be filled with zany folks—not much room for animals, especially the boring ones. The stars in the night sky hold no interest for advertisers, for they don't reflect us. The stars that *do* reflect us are the kind that appear on talk shows. Since we can't all appear on TV, our race needs some representatives, and these are the people filling the couch next to Regis and Kelly. If they were of interest because they were actors, Jay Leno would ask them questions about acting— "How did you conjure up the mood for that scene?" Instead, we want to know about their lives, and the lives of other stars they have "worked with." They are of interest because they are stand-ins for us. By the very act of being important, they redeem the lifetime we spend watching them. Most cultures, historically, have put something else—God or nature or some combination—at the center. But we've put these things at the periphery. A consumer society doesn't need them to function, and it can't tolerate the limits they might impose; there's only need for people. *Most cultures, historically, have put something else—God or nature or some combination—at the center. But we've put these things at the periphery. A consumer society doesn't need them to function, and it can't tolerate the limits they might impose; there's only need for people.* Our culture is a natural extension, magnified a thousand times, of the culture that Job and his friends inhabited; it revolves entirely around us, leaving very little room for anything else.

The most common way of describing our lives in this more humble world is "stewardship"—it's certainly the word we've usually hit on in recent years to describe the biblically sanctioned relationship between people and the earth. It is a useful idea, in no small measure because it's hard to argue with. No one stands up and declares that they think we should be bad stewards of the land. But this of course is also its weakness—the idea of "stewardship" is so lacking in content as to give us very little guidance about how to behave in any given situation. (In fact, many of the worst stewards of the earth are the most vociferous in talking about stewardship.) It's as if we said that our faith instructs us to be "good" to other people, or to be "kind" to them, or to treat them "nicely." It does, of course, but that doesn't get us very far. Is it good to give people what they need for survival, or is it good to deny them those things so that they will get tough and learn to shift for themselves? Is it good to turn the other cheek, or to hit back so that they learn to leave others alone? These are the sort of questions that are fleshed out throughout the Bible—"good" is given some content. And so is stewardship. It is not long before we begin to run across some of the familiar sanctions that start to shape the experience of stewardship. For instance, the idea of the sabbatical year and the jubilee year have the effect of resting the land and also of preventing the consolidation of the land into what we would now call "agribusiness" farms—the massive industrial spreads that accelerate all the soil erosion and pesticide poisoning and monoculture reliance that are ruining the earth. And we are cautioned in Isaiah, "Woe to you who add house to house and join field to field, till no space is left and you live alone in the land," a warning that the "developers" of our day and age have sadly not heeded. We read in Numbers that town planners are to leave a belt of open space one thousand cubits wide all around the city. There are regulations about when plowing is allowable, which Torah scholars assure us were remarkably sensitive to issues like the height of the water table.

All these examples of stewardship are useful to us as we consider the choices posed by many situations. They call, in general, for human restraint—there is an emphasis not on immediate gratification, but on the long-term survival of the productivity and integrity of the land. If the people of the Mediterranean had followed their advice, they would not have turned much of that area into the treeless desert it currently is. If we followed their advice, we would take great care not to erode our topsoil—not to fritter away in a generation or two the careful accumulation of millennia on which our breakfasts, lunches, and dinners depend. We would not cut down rain forests for the sake of a few years' profit, nor overfish the oceans for the sake of this season's payoff. The people of the Old Testament recognized much better than we recognize that there was an endless cycle at work, and that if it wasn't abused it would support us quite nicely. They were ecologically sensible. However, most of these conclusions might be arrived at without the aid of the Scriptures, relying instead on common sense alone. Though we continue to do so, it clearly makes no sense to work soil until it is exhausted, to supplement it with fertilizers and poisons till it is robbed of all health, to let it wash away with the rain. It clearly makes no sense to continue sprawling our suburbs out across the landscape, joining lot to lot in an endless agglomeration of sterile houses pleasing neither to the eye nor to the soul which rob us of community and force our dependence on wasteful forms of transportation. It clearly makes no sense to cut our forests faster than they will grow back, and to clear-cut them in such a way that the old and balanced mix of species will never return. We shouldn't need the Bible to tell us these things—they are common sense. But common sense applies a certain set of values to any question—usually a utilitarian set of values. It is stupid to let the soil erode because it won't be there in the future when we need it to grow food. It is stupid to cut down trees faster than they can grow because we'll run out. These utilitarian values are usually rooted in the question, "What's best for us?" It is a far better question than "What's best for me?" but stills falls short, I think, of both theological and ecological demands. What we need to be figuring out, in this time of crisis, is nothing less than what the proper relationship is between people, the earth, and God.

And that, to me, involves the second great point of the voice from the whirlwind. That voice does not confine its remarks to the propositions "You are small and I am large," or "I am old and you are an infant." It does not speak to us in purely rational terms. It does not call us only to humility.

The voice also calls us, overwhelmingly, to joy. To immersion in the fantastic beauty and drama all around us. It does not call us to think, to categorize, to analyze, to evaluate. It calls us to be. The reason Job matters so much to me is because of the language—the biologically accurate, earthy, juicy, crusty, *wild*, untamed poetry of God's great speech. Now, commentators—mostly urban commentators, I would wager—have insisted over the centuries that God's answer is obscure; I read recently an interview with a leading rock hard fundamentalist who believed every word in the Bible, but said that he thought the language in Job was probably "poetic." Many others have said that simply the presence of God alone is answer enough for Job. But that is absurd, if only because of the incredible strength that the artist lavishes on his words. We are to listen to God with that part of us that is most open to the power of art. Not just our ears—more than anything, the images are visual, sensual, a total contrast to the gnat-straining and wool-gathering and other academic exercises that have occupied the previous thirty chapters. God doesn't even deign to dismiss all that talk as vain. No—he simply embarks on a defiantly proud tour of the physical world, a world filled with untamed glory that reflects his own:

> Do you hunt game for the lioness
>   and feed her ravenous cubs,
> when they crouch in their den, impatient,
>   or lie in ambush in the thicket?
> Who finds her prey at nightfall,
>   when her cubs are aching with hunger?

This, remember, came in a day before lions were confined to game preserves and people drove up in jeeps to stare at them—this was in a day when lions were a real threat to people. And yet beloved of God. Provided for by God. When I read that it makes me tremble to think of my mountains of New York, where only a century ago you could still find mountain lion. And it is not just the fierce that God boasts about, but the disgusting as well.

> Do you teach the vulture to soar
>   and build his nest in the clouds?
> He makes his home on the mountaintop,
>   on the unapproachable crag.
> He sits and scans for prey;
>   from far off his eyes can spot it;
> his little ones drink its blood.
>   Where the unburied are, he is.

Job complains that the world makes no sense and God shows him the little vultures drinking blood. That is his answer—little vultures drinking blood. We are beyond categories here, and into the rich, tough, gristly fabric of life. God shows Job the ostrich, too, silliest of all creatures:

> Do you deck the ostrich with wings,
>> with elegant plumes and feathers?
> She lays her eggs in the dirt
>> and lets them hatch on the ground,
> forgetting that a foot may crush them
>> or sharp teeth crack them open.
> She treats her children cruelly,
>> as if they were not her own.
> For God deprived her of wisdom
>> and left her with little sense.
> [And yet] *when she spreads her wings to run,*
>> *she laughs at the horse and rider.* [Emphasis added]

That sense of ebullient, shivery wildness runs throughout this whole poem—the "foolish" ostrich redeemed by her pure speed, her pure laughing speed. This is not the tame and citified vision of the lion lying down with the lamb—it is a rapacious, tough, deadly, amoral, glorious wildness.

> Do you give the horse his strength?
>> Do you clothe his neck with terror?
> Do you make him leap like a locust,
>> snort like a blast of thunder?
> He paws and champs at the bit;
>> he exults as he charges into battle.
> He laughs at the sight of danger;
>> he does not wince from the sword
> or the arrows nipping at his ears
>> or the flash of spear and javelin.
> With his hooves he swallows the ground;
>> he quivers at the sound of the trumpet.

Wildness is such a gift, a gift worth suffering for:

> Who unties the wild ass
>> and lets him wander at will?
> He ranges the open prairie
>> and roams across the saltlands.
> He is far from the tumult of cities;

> he laughs at the driver's whip.
> He scours the hills for food,
> > in search of anything green.

The tenderness of that last line—the hungry ass, scouring the desert hills for food and yet laughing at the order and security represented by the stable. The meaning is clear—it is overpowering. Not only are all these things mighty and inexplicable and painful, but they are unbearably beautiful to God. They are right. They should brew in us a fierce and intoxicating joy.

> Do you tell the antelope to calve
> > or ease her when she is in labor?
> Do you count the months of her fullness
> > and know when her time has come?
> She kneels; she tightens her womb;
> > she pants, she presses, gives birth.
> Her little ones grow up;
> > they leave and never return.

It is not a storybook that we were born into, but a rich and complicated novel without any conclusion. Every page of this novel speaks of delight—not rational, painless, comfortable, easy pleasure, but delight.

The passages I have cited are the first great piece of modern nature writing, cutting through all the romance and fear and psychological nonsense that people have piled on to the woods and mountains. Millennia passed before that tone completely reemerged, perhaps most clearly in the writing of John Muir. The year after Muir took his long walk to the Gulf of Mexico which I have already described, he found his way to California—and in fact to Yosemite, where he spent a summer wandering the high country. He climbed all the mountains, swam all the lakes, and spent hours in rapt contemplation of clouds and squirrels and incense cedars. Once again we have his journal, and this time he has escaped his wrestlings with his father's Calvinism and emerged into the full-blown presence of the divine. There is no more ecstatic book I have ever read—it compares with the accounts left behind by saints of their fervent happiness in prayer. Muir opens himself to the whole world, bathes in the unbelievable beauty and *righteousness* of the pristine world of the high Sierra. June 20—"The air is distinctly fragrant with balsam and resin and mint—every breath of it a gift we may well thank God for. Who could ever guess that so rough a wilderness should yet be so fine, so full of good things. One seems to be in a majestic domed pavilion in which a grand play is being acted with scenery and music and incense—all the furniture and action so interesting we are in no danger of being called on to endure one dull moment. God himself seems to be always doing his best here, working like a man in a glow of enthusiasm." June 23—"Oh, these vast calm measureless mountain days, inciting at once to work and rest! Days in whose light everything seems equally divine, opening a thousand windows to show us God. Nevermore, however weary, should one faint by the way who gains the blessings of one mountain day; whatever his fate, long life, short life, stormy or calm, he is rich forever." August 13—and excuse me for the length of this excerpt, but it captures the wild joy of Muir's summer. "The forests seem kindly familiar, and the lakes and meadows and glad singing streams. I should like to dwell with them forever. Here with bread and water I should be content. Even if not allowed to roam and climb, tethered to a stake or tree in some meadow or grove, even then I should be content forever. Bathed in such beauty, watching the expressions ever varying on the faces of the mountains, watching the stars which here have a glory that the lowlander never dreams of, watching the circling seasons, listening to the songs of the waters and winds and birds, would be endless pleasure. And what glorious cloud-lands I should see, storms and calms—a new heaven and a new earth every day, aye and new inhabitants. I feel sure I should not have one dull moment. And why should this appear extravagant? It is only common sense, a sign of health, genuine, natural, all-awake health. One would be at an endless Godful play, and what speeches and music and acting and scenery and lights!—sun, moon, stars, auroras. Creation just beginning, the morning stars still 'singing together and all the sons of God shouting for joy.'"

I spent one recent summer in the backcountry of Yosemite, repairing damaged trails, and for ten glorious days we had not a drop of rain, just the cool, bright, eternally fresh world Muir describes. But it's important to realize that this ecstatic world exists everywhere around us that has not been fully tamed. I lived in New York City for a number of years, and I used to spend a great deal of time in the outdoors. Prospect Park in Brooklyn is one of those Frederick Law Olmstead marvels, but it has fallen on hard times—badly maintained, filled with the sad men of the city. I used to run a small homeless shelter, and I would go to visit some of my clients there in the park, but eventually I would stray to the pond in the middle. And there, hidden in the weeds, oblivious of the drug deals and street fights, I would always find some treasure—a green heron, or one time a loon that had strayed off course on the spring migration and taken a rest in the pond. One of the few remaining patches of green along that section of the eastern flyway, it was a birdwatcher's paradise. Further out, on the industrial margins of Brooklyn and Queens, there were grimy beaches that ran for miles beside the highways. And for a few weeks each spring those beaches crawled with horseshoe crabs—tens of thousands of them coming ashore to mate, as they had in that same place for eons. Horseshoe crabs link us with a distant, mythic time—they are so unchanged that they retain copper-based blood instead of iron. This ancient, impassive invasion of fertility always moved me to no end, in part I think because of the debt I owe Muir. His ecstatic vision has done much to shape the environmental movement in this country, and therefore the world—most of all he has given us the grammar of joy, the lens of wildness, through which many of us perceive the planet. But it is vital to note that Muir is not some ecstatic precursor of New Agers. It is true that his separation from the physical world falls away in his ecstasy—he feels himself a part of the world—that is his glory. But he does not fall into the trap of thinking the whole world is in *him*. His great gift is humility, radical humility. Many people, he wrote while in the Florida swamps, "believe the alligators were created by the Devil, thus accounting for their all-consuming appetite and ugliness. But doubtless these creatures are happy and fill the place assigned for them by the great Creator of us all. Fierce and cruel they appear to us, but beautiful in the eyes of God." And then he addresses the gators: "Honorable representatives of the great saurians of older creation, may you long enjoy your lilies and rushes, and be blessed now and then with a mouthful of terror-stricken man by way of dainty!" And note again that when Muir wrote this he was camped in a swamp.

This kind of untamed joy, of rapture, is not confined to our dealings with the natural world, of course. Friendship, love, sex—all are openings into this irrational and deeply moving world. None move solely according to the calculations we are taught by the economists and advertisers; all produce joy far deeper than any material acquisition. Sometimes it seems even as if the most irrational behaviors produce the most satisfaction. As I mentioned, I ran a small homeless shelter for a while from my church in New York. I spent many nights there, spraying Lysol, delousing sheets, making beds, mopping floors, cooking stew. By any rational calculation this should have represented "sacrifice," giving up the pleasure of my own pursuits. But of course, as all who have done such things (and most people have done more than I have) know, the work is essentially selfish, for it provides intense, quiet pleasure. It is, I think, the same pleasure that Muir observed in Yosemite—the joy of immersion in something outside yourself, something larger than yourself. I have felt the same kind of thing in the natural world myself, an acceptance that convenience and comfort and ease are secondary goals at best, and sometimes very much in the way of actual experience of the world's glory. One summer recently I was hiking in the Adirondack Mountains where I live, three or four days into a wet solo backpacking trip. It was a spongy saturated dawn, and I emerged a little later than usual from my tent deep in Cold River country. I ate my oatmeal, packed my sack, and stumbled off south along the trail, the brush and branches soaking my trousers with their load of last night's rain. I hadn't gone far when I turned a corner and walked into a doe. She looked at me and I looked at her, not ten feet away—we kept it up for ten minutes, till finally I wandered off. A mile further on, in the first deep woods past Shattuck Clearing, a hawk hung on a branch eighteen inches above my hat, peering quizzically down. He was in no hurry either—the misty chill was making everyone reluctant to move, either that or I was giving off peaceful vibrations. (Or maybe—magic thought—after a week of hiking by myself perhaps I was sending out no vibrations at all.)

As I walked, I kept coming across new mushrooms, extravagant neon forms and half-obscene profusions that were the particular glory of that damp year—glistening folds of chocolate slime, tree shelves the color of traffic cones, pustulant acnes of puffballs spreading down the spines of fallen hemlocks. I camped early, stopping in an afternoon drizzle at a private spot on the eastern edge of Long Lake, but I'd hardly fired the stove for tea when the sun began to carve rifts in the mist, portholes that looked out on the blue sky above. The holes grew fast; soon a week's worth of clammy socks hung from pine branches and I was sitting on a rock by water's edge, toasting my pale, wrinkled feet. And the Disney movie continued: a family of mergansers and then a brace of loon swam by within spitting distance. As it darkened that evening, a beaver slid by my dangling toes. Later, at the absolute corner of can't-see, a heron floated in to the beach where I sat and stalked in the shallows till she had her fill. She left, I slept—and by midnight the stars had vanished, the rain had returned, and my socks were wet once more. The next day I saw some chipmunks. But a whiff of that wilderness lingered in my nose, mixing with the tang left from all the other times I've smelled it—wet, dusty, rank, crackling, mushy days, bear days and eagle days, bee-stung and loon-sung days. This nonrational world of smells and sounds and sights, of immersion, of smallness and quietness, answers to some of our deepest yearnings.

* * *

The challenge before us is to figure out how to link these two callings, these two imperatives from the voice in the whirlwind—the call to humility and the call to joy. Each one, on its own, is insufficient. Humility by itself is an arid negativism; a gleeful communion with the earth around us can turn quickly into some New Age irresponsibility, where we come to identify the cosmos with us and not vice-versa. But together they are reinforcing, powerful—powerful enough, perhaps, to start changing some of the deep-seated behaviors that are driving our environmental destruction, our galloping poverty, our cultural despair. And fortunately the two can go hand in hand.

I talked before about the need for a bicycle-based transit system for cities and suburbs. Then the context was environmental—we need to make this shift rather than continue to fill the air with automobile emissions. It was a necessary humility we needed to practice quickly. But riding a bike has other advantages, too—quantum increases in joy. You are outside, with the breeze and the sun. Your pace allows you to actually see your surroundings, to stop and talk with your neighbors, and therefore it helps turn a place into a community, rich with texture and interaction. The amount of information about the world that you absorb jumps tremendously—you notice topography, for instance, because you need to do more than decline your ankle an extra degree to make it up a hill. And you feel your body again—feel the strain in your calves, the pump in your chest, the strength in your arms. You feel your own wildness. We realize instinctively that we want our bodies to work, to move, to stretch, but we choose such strange ways of showing it. We drive to the health spa, pay someone a large sum of money, and climb aboard a stationary bicycle. Instead we must learn to integrate our joy into our lives.

The church or synagogue or mosque can be an enormous help in this task of integration. In fact, religious institutions are for two reasons better situated than any other force in our society to help us make these kinds of changes. The first is because they are the only institution left in society that understands some goal other than material progress—that can see a point to human life other than "The one who has the most things when he dies, wins." Traditionally, of course, there has been great praise for humility among the religious, and if it has been more in theory than in practice, at least the theory is sound. The second reason that the churches could be so important is because they understand better than any other institution the possibilities of *transcendent* joy. At their best, they stand outside the consumer society. (Though those of us who have had the opportunity to watch six religious channels around the clock can testify that there are plenty of exceptions, including one nationally syndicated preacher who appeared with an enormous facsimile check, like the ones they give to lottery winners, which had been drawn

on the Bank of Heaven and signed by Jesus Christ himself.)
Fellowship, service, a deep relationship with God—these are the
sorts of joys that the churches can cultivate.

I want to describe just one small project that combines these
two challenges, the call to humility and the call to joy. In the
1990s, the Troy Conference of the United Methodist Church,
which covers northern New York and the state of Vermont,
passed a resolution urging its 80,000 members to try to limit their
Christmas gift spending to one hundred dollars per family. It
began, frankly, as an effort to address environmental and social
problems—as a call to humility. Surely, we reasoned, the church
had a right to advise its members how to celebrate a religious holiday. And surely our region would be better off if some of the vast
resources spent at the mall in mid-December were diverted to
other uses. As we researched it, the scale of Christmas in America
surprised even us. Each Christmas morning, Americans open
nearly $40 billion in presents, a figure that exceeds not only the
gross national product of Ireland but also the total charitable giving by individual Americans to all charities the entire year. The
average American spends something like $700 on Christmas pres-
ents. Only one-quarter manage to stick to a budget, and more
than a fifth take better than four months to pay off their bills,
meaning their last Christmas is paid for about the time the first
catalogues arrive for the next one. Where I live, in a cold and
poor mountain region, it means that people very often cannot
pay their January fuel bills because of the pressure to have a
"proper Christmas." Some of the environmental impact of this
holiday should be obvious—the energy and resources consumed
in creating items that are not necessary, the thousands of square
miles of wrapping paper, even the harvest of batteries that soon
will end up in the trash. On a deeper level, it seems likely that
Christmas serves as the best school of materialism that anyone
could ask for—the fanatic attention paid by children to the
growing stack of gifts, the shrieking moment of excess as the
paper flies, the total identification of joy with consumption.
This lesson has even spread to other cultures: though less than
one percent of the Japanese, for instance, are Christians,

Christmas gift giving has become an enormous preoccupation. Any possible spiritual component is obscured—one large Tokyo department store recently featured an enormous display window of a crucified Santa.

But all those are, in some sense, negative reasons for changing the Christmas celebration. They are responses to the call to humility, but as we thought more and talked more about Christmas we realized that they were only half the reasons to change. The other set of reasons were answers to the call to joy. As almost everyone will admit, the approach of the Christmas season causes a certain amount of dread as well as anticipation. Even for those with money enough to pull off a "proper" Christmas, there is always the lurking fear that they won't get the right present, or spend enough, or spend too much. The rush, the confusion, the endless shopping—all get in the way of the season. So we decided to concentrate our "Hundred Dollar Holiday" campaign not on the need to spend less money but on the need to have more joy. The poster we designed for the occasions says nothing about environmental or social problems; we find most people are already convinced about these issues. Instead, it offers a long list of alternative gifts to make that both downplay materialism and allow for deeper connections between people. For instance: grandparents can tape themselves reading a favorite book and then send the book and the tape to the grandchild who can play it over and over again; old jewelry can be cleaned and passed on, perhaps with a card that describes some great event where it was worn; people can give each other trips to the museum or coupons for backrubs or a dozen different ideas. And with the church sanctioning these practices, it becomes easier for people to resist the social and commercial pressures to buy.

Which is not to say that the campaign has been entirely easy—no change away from the old orthodoxies ever is. We've been attacked by conservative columnists and business groups for undermining the economy, and even called Scrooges. But the answers are fairly simple, and they seem to have been persuasive to many. Surely diverting money currently spent on electronic tie racks and net-linked Xboxes to savings accounts or to basic human needs can't be bad for the economy—our "crushing debt burden" is regularly invoked as a cause for the malaise of the early 1990s. And surely the real Scrooges, the people taking the fun out of Christmas, are the advertisers who assert that without this toy and that appliance it won't be a real Christmas. We've hosted a series of evening meetings, alive with folk music and gospel choirs and storytellers, and we have listened as one person after another says "I've always wanted to do something like this, but I never felt like I could."

All the ideas we have for Christmas gifts—from following Saint Francis's lead and scattering seed on Christmas morning so the birds, too, can share in the joy of the Nativity to the simple, timeless act of baking good bread for friends and relatives—share in common an immersion in the real world, a step back from the manipulated and commercial society in which we find ourselves so firmly stuck. They come as a shock, much as the voice from the whirlwind shocked Job; perhaps they will help shock some of us out of our narrow preoccupations and into the real drama and joys that the planet provides. "I had heard of you with my ears; / but now my eyes have seen you," Job tells God at the very end of his great speech. But of course he hadn't seen God, only a disembodied voice from a whirlwind. What he had seen was the glory spread out around us, available to each of us whenever we care to look with new eyes instead of the blinders of old orthodoxy.

CHAPTER

3

Glory surely shone round on every side, and for Job, this glory was enough. It seemed quite literally to fill him up, to leave no breath for the bellowing that had been his trademark throughout the story. "I am speechless: what can I answer?" he said. "I put my hand on my mouth. / I have said too much already; / now I will speak no more." It is not simply his smallness in the face of the infinite that shuts him up, it is his sense that that infinity is somehow sufficient. "I had heard of you with my ears; / but now my eyes have seen you. / Therefore I will be quiet, *comforted* that I am dust" [emphasis added].

In times previous, this was enough. The answer of God to Job represented a timeless message for human beings about who we were. And because it was timeless, it was easy to ignore its most obvious and plain meaning in practice. It was all right to kill the lions where we were—there were more lions somewhere else to roar God's glory. But now we come to a wickedly hard moment when the message is not self-evident—when it is no longer clear that we will always be smaller than God, at least in physical terms. We have about run out of lions. We must make stark choices, and depending on how we choose it is possible that the earthy, breathing voice from the whirlwind will become at best metaphysical, and at worst an odd echo from some earlier "primitive" time.

To feel in one's gut the dimensions of this tragedy, it is necessary to return to the beginning of God's speech, which consists of a series of questions the answers to which in all other times must have seemed self-evident. Grand, booming, sarcastic questions, designed to make Job feel small. And successfully. What could he say when God asked,

> Where were you when I planned the earth?
> Tell me, if you are so wise.
> Do you know who took its dimensions,
> measuring its length with a cord?
> What were its pillars built on?
> Who laid down its cornerstone,
> while the morning stars burst out singing
> and the angels shouted for joy!

Job had to stand silent, to admit that he could not answer. And so must we—even our grandest science seems destined not to penetrate that first morning, to understand the pillars and the cornerstone. We stand in awe before that dawn when the very stars sang out in wonder—so far so good. But God continues,

> Were you there when I stopped the waters,
> as they issued gushing from the womb?
> when I wrapped the ocean in clouds
> and swaddled the sea in shadows?
> when I closed it in with barriers
> and set its boundaries, saying,
> "Here you may come, but no farther;
> here shall your proud waves break."

Again Job must stand in mute silence. But what about us? As I explained earlier, we as a civilization are on the verge of changing the boundaries of the ocean, the place where the proud waves break. Any increase in global average temperature will likely raise sea level. Researchers do not expect a science-fiction surge—the Antarctic ice shelves are actually quite stable, reducing the possibility that the Empire State Building will be immersed to the fortieth floor. More likely, a little melting of polar ice and glaciers will combine with the thermal expansion of warm water (which takes up more space than cold) to raise the sea level two or three feet. Increases of this magnitude might well be enough to wipe out half the coastal marshes and wetlands on this continent, the most biologically productive parts of the ocean. These marshes won't be able to migrate inland both because the rise will happen too quickly, and because inland on this continent and many other places we have built strings of highways, chains of beach houses. A rise of one foot on a beach of average slope brings the ocean ninety feet inland, which in some cases is right to the road. Plans are already in the works for dikes to protect these structures. But there are some things we can't build dikes for. I was recently in the Maldive Islands, an archipelago in the Indian Ocean. They are absolutely beautiful islands, more than fifteen hundred in number, most no bigger than the size of a football field. They are ringed by gorgeous reefs, and the people who live there are traditionally ecologically conscious—they fish with handlines instead of nets, for instance, to avoid depleting marine stocks. The only hitch in this paradise is that the highest point in the whole archipelago is about six feet above sea level. A rise of a meter would mean that every storm would wash across the inhabitants—the islands would be unoccupied. This is not God's power—this is our power: our cars, our factories, our burning rain forests.

> If you shout commands to the thunderclouds,
> > will they rush off to do your bidding?
> If you clap for the bolts of lightning,
> > will they come and say "Here we are"?
> Who gathers up the stormclouds,
> > slits them and pours them out,
> turning dust to mud
> > and soaking the cracked clay?

Who indeed. By altering the global average temperature we will alter the circulation patterns of weather, changing dramatically the places and amounts of rain that fall. In general, there may be increased precipitation, because warmer air can hold more water vapor. However, most of the computer models indicate that this decrease will be more than offset by increased evaporation from the warmer temperatures. The numbers are staggering—virgin flows along the Colorado, for instance, could fall fifty percent by the middle of the next century on a river that is already over-stretched by the demands of Westerners. Or consider this: A study described in *Nature* magazine by a team of Canadian researchers focused on three lakes in northern Ontario. Over the last two decades the average temperature of those lakes had climbed 3.5 degrees—not necessarily because of the greenhouse effect, but at the very least a vivid analogue of what we can expect. Around those three lakes, evaporation had increased and therefore the flows of the streams that fed them fell—with less organic material coming into the ponds, they became much clearer, meaning sunlight could penetrate further, warming the water. At the same time, increased forest fires had decreased tree cover around the area, which in turn meant higher winds—these too drove the cold water layer much deeper into the lake. Together, these pushed cold water fish like trout to the brink of extirpation. God did not do this—we did this. And we're doing more of it all the time. The latest numbers from the CO_2 recorder on the side of Mauna Loa shows that annual increases in carbon dioxide are now pushing two parts per million, the highest ever recorded. Some scientists think it's a sign that the forests of the northern hemisphere are losing their capacity to serve as a carbon sink.

> Have you seen where the snow is stored
>   or visited the storehouse of hail,
> which I keep for the day of terror,
>   the final hours of the world?
>
> Where is the west wind released
>   and the east wind sent down to earth?

If anything seems like an act of God it is a hurricane—Job, of course, has no idea how to answer this set of questions. We, unfortunately, are learning more. The strongest winds on earth are in essence stored in the heat in the upper layers of the world's oceans—the warmer those layers, the stronger hurricanes can come. At current temperatures—at God-set temperatures—the winds of a hurricane like Andrew were about as strong as physically possible—a little over two hundred miles per hour. If you raise sea surface temperatures even a few degrees, though, top winds might increase by as much as fifty miles per hour—and since the destructiveness of hurricane winds is geometrically, not linearly, related to their speed, this would mean hurricanes perhaps twice as dangerous. This is not God's doing—we are doing this, every time we press on the accelerator or turn up the thermostat or consume something we don't require.

What we are doing is very simple—we are taking over control of the physical world around us. The most basic laws remain beyond our grasp—gravity still causes objects to fall, atoms still repel at close distances, the sun still revolves around the earth. But nature on the scale immediately and constantly visible to us—the world of animals, of rainfall, of trees, of waves—may soon answer to us, as our crude alterations of atmospheric chemistry begin to guide the most fundamental processes of terrestrial life. Forgive me if I describe an experience that I described once before, in my book *The End of Nature*. It takes place during a walk down the creek that runs by my house, a lovely stream that falls through the woods for about fifteen miles before it flows into the widening Hudson. This passage was written at the foot of the biggest waterfall along the way: "Changing socks in front of the waterfall, I thought back to the spring before last, when a record snowfall melted in only a dozen or so warm April days. A little to the south, an inflamed stream washed out a highway bridge, closing the New York Thruway for months. Mill Creek filled till it was a river, and this waterfall, normally one of those diaphonous-veil affairs, turned into a cataract. It filled me with awe to stand there then, on the shaking ground, and think, This is what nature is capable of.

"But as I sat there this time and thought about the dry summer we'd just come through, there was nothing awe-inspiring or instructive or even lulling in the fall of the water. It suddenly seemed less like a waterfall than like a spillway to accommodate the overflow of a reservoir. That didn't decrease its beauty, but it changed its meaning. It has begun or will soon begin to rain and snow when the particular mix of chemicals we've injected into the atmosphere adds up to rain or snow—when they make it hot enough over some tropical sea to form a cloud and send it this way. I had no more control, in one sense, over this process than I ever did. But it felt different, and lonelier. Instead of a world where rain had an independent and mysterious existence, the rain had become a subset of human activity: a phenomenon like smog or commerce or the noise from the skidder hauling logs out by the road—all things over which I had no control either. The rain bore a brand: it was a steer, not a deer. And that was where the loneliness came from. There's nothing there except us.

"The walk along Mill Creek, or any stream, or up any hill, or through any woods, is changed forever—changed as profoundly as when it shifted from pristine and untracked wilderness to mapped and deeded and cultivated land. Our local shopping mall now has a club of people who go 'mall walking' every day. They circle the shopping center en masse—Caldor to Sears to J.C. Penney, circuit after circuit with an occasional break to shop. This seems less absurd to me than it did at first. I like to walk in the outdoors not solely because the air is cleaner, but because outdoors we venture into a sphere larger than ourselves. Mall walking involves too many other people, and too many purely human sights, ever to be more than good-natured exercise. But now, out in the wild, the sunshine on one's shoulders is a reminder that man has cracked the ozone, that, thanks to us, the atmosphere absorbs where once it released. The greenhouse effect is a more apt name than those who coined it imagined. The carbon dioxide and trace gases act like the panes of glass in a greenhouse—the analogy is accurate. But it's more than that. We have built a greenhouse, *a human creation*, where once there bloomed a sweet and wild garden."

Such changes may not be "unnatural," in the sense that we are part of nature. But they clearly mark theological and philosophical differences that all of us intuitively recognize. If you are camped by some wilderness lake watching the sunset and you look down at the shore and see a collection of McDonald's sacks and beer bottles bobbing in the waves, you do not think to yourself, "This is just like deer droppings." You feel—unless you are the cretin that put them there in the first place—less like you fit in. You feel like a part of a race that has not learned enough about humility. And in the decades ahead those McDonald's sacks and beer bottles may be *everywhere*—invisible, it is true, but carbon dioxide is litter even more profound than a Pepsi can.

Furthermore, we are challenging God's control over creation in deliberate as well as inadvertent ways. At the same precise moment that we are stepping over the greenhouse threshold, we are crossing another barrier—the wall of genetic integrity that had always severely limited our ability to modify the life forms around us.

> Is your arm like the arm of God?
>> Can your voice bellow like mine? . . .
> Look now: the Beast that I made:
>> he eats grass like a bull.
> Look: the power in his thighs,
>> the pulsing sinews of his belly.
> His penis stiffens like a pine;
>> his testicles bulge with vigor.
> His ribs are bars of bronze,
>> his bones iron beams.
> He is first of the works of God,
>> created to be my plaything.

Or consider the other brute animal God describes:

> He sneezes and lightnings flash;
>> his eyes glow like dawn.
> Smoke pours from his nostrils
>> like steam from a boiling pot.
> His breath sets coals ablaze;
>> flames leap from his mouth.
> Power beats in his neck,
>> and terror dances before him.
> His skin is hard as a rock,
>> his heart huge as a boulder.

I do not mean here to enter the age-old debate over the identity of Behemoth and Leviathan—they are clearly designed to give the impression, among others, of a deity who can create as he pleases. What is important for us to understand is that as a species our arms *are* increasingly like the arms of God. Our fields are now filled with transgenic corn and soybeans and cotton, and our labs boast cloned sheep, "smart" mice, even rabbits crossed with jellyfish genes so they glow green in the dark. My 2003 book *Enough: Staying Human in an Engineered Age* catalogues such curiosities, and catalogues as well the desire of some researchers, like the Nobelist James Watson, to extend the work to humans, improving human embryos so they wouldn't be "stupid" or "ugly" or "shy."

Some have said that such work is merely an extension of selective breeding, a practice almost as old as human beings. But this is not the case. Selective breeding could be carried on only within narrowly defined limits. You could not induce a pig to share genes with a pine. The limits of selective breeding helped define the boundaries of any species. What we are now engaged in is something different—a process of ending all limits. Researchers peering ahead a few decades were talking about "growing" chickens on assembly lines fed with nutrient broth with no need for the "inefficient" heads and wings. Eventually, said one writer, all plants might "become unnecessary," replaced by artificial leaves that would "waste" none of the sunlight they receive on luxuries like roots and flowers but instead use "all the energy they trap to make things for us to use." Instead of being used in the most limited of ways—to treat childhood diseases, say—genetic engineering will, in the words of one British author, soon "enable us to turn the working of all living things on earth—the entire biosphere—to the particular advantage of our own species." Listen to that phrase again: "turn the working of all living things on earth—the entire biosphere—to the particular advantage of our own species."

The problem is not that some monster is going to escape from the laboratory and kill us all—the problem is that the monster of our own egos is going to be reflected in everything around us. The world will become a shopping mall, everything designed for our delectation. Like God we will build creatures to be our "playthings." But I doubt if they will be as wonderful, as variegated, or as wild as the creatures of the first creation. The characteristics we want—efficiency, cheapness, standardization—would never produce the exuberant abundance we find around us. Peacocks don't come from planners, nor armadillos from accountants. If we leave our footprints over every inch of the planet, if we redesign its plants and animals solely to suit us—than we spit in the face of God. We can match his sarcasm with ours. "Were you there when I stopped the waters / as they issued gushing from the womb? / . . . when I closed [the ocean] in with barriers / and set its boundaries. . . ?" won't sound so mighty. It will sound like some old geezer. Screw off, Grandpop—we do all that stuff now, and more. We set the boundaries of the forests—no more beech trees in the lower forty-eight. That coral you're always talking about—we got rid of that. Behemoth? Leviathan? Give me a break—we're building them twice as big now. The drive for human power and control that began in Eden is gaining an unstoppable momentum, and we are making that same choice with each day that passes.

Much of this genetic work is being done to solve environmental problems—or, rather, to work around environmental problems that we have no intention of solving. For instance, scientists are hard at work on crop species better able to withstand prolonged bouts of high temperatures, of the sort the computer modelers predict will soon afflict us. Others are working out technological solutions to global environmental problems—ferrying fleetloads of chemicals to the upper stratosphere in an effort to reverse the greenhouse effect, or designing satellites that might cast perfectly geometrical, enormous shadows over the planet.

It is possible that such measures might "work"—that they might stabilize certain physical systems to allow our species to survive, at least for a while longer, with our present habits and economies. They are the equivalent of building a plastic bubble over the planet—or over the rich portion of the planet, anyhow, for of course the genetically engineered plants won't be affordable for developing world peasants, and the extensive dikes already planned to help the coastal United States cope with the sea level rise won't do much for the residents of Bangladesh, the vast majority of them crowded onto the flood plain at ocean's edge. Forget for a moment the issue of justice, however, and consider the proposition in purely selfish terms. Do we want to live on a space station? For that is what it would be—a human creation, where we regulate as best we can the physical systems around us, entirely for our own best interest. A *managed* world.

If we build this world that I fear—this world where every rainstorm speaks of our habits, where the oceans rise and fall reflecting our indulgence, where creatures mirror our whims and fashions—the sadness will mostly be ours, I suppose. Later generations don't remember what we know—they'll be better adjusted than I am, not so angry. They will not know what they are missing. If we manage to wipe out the grizzly bear by wiping out Yellowstone, or if, as some have suggested, we genetically alter him so he will no longer be aggressive, then no one will ever feel the peculiar and intensely alive alertness of a walk though wild North America. Soon that idea will fade, and the Disneyland mantra—safe, clean, predictable—will be absolutely unchallenged in anyone's mind.

But I have a feeling that even if later generations are better adjusted they may be less likely to go to church. I want to speak from the self-interest of religious communities for a little while, for I fear very much that this new world we are building will be even less hospitable to our religious message than the current one. It is no accident that most world religions have grown, in the beginning, from an attempt to explain the phenomena of the physical world. I was recently in Hawaii, doing some research on the largest rain forest in the United States, a rain forest that is being systematically destroyed to make way for a geothermal power plant. This rain forest was on the edge of a volcano, Kilaeua, which is the largest active volcano in America. I stood and watched the lava flow into the Pacific, building a new island. And I stood and talked with the Hawaiian natives who have lived there for generations—quite understandably they believe in a volcano god Pele. Why wouldn't they? They live surrounded by smoke and sulfur. And, incidentally, that strong belief has fueled their strong efforts to save the rain forest, an effort in which the local Christian churches have not been conspicuous. We have insulated ourselves to some degree from nature. We live away from volcanoes, and even from forests and mountains. We don't grow much of our food. Still, the images of God's power that help us locate ourselves on an axis with the divine come largely from nature. It is no accident that many of the best-loved hymns of our faith draw on this emotional power—"O Lord my God, when I in awesome wonder / Consider all the works thy hands hath made / I see the stars, I hear the rolling thunder / Thy pow'r throughout the universe displayed / Then sings my soul, my Savior God to thee / How Great Thou Art, How Great Thou Art." When Christ prays hardest, where does he go? To the temple? No—to the wilderness or to the garden. The point is, faith in some larger-than-human force requires evidence of it at work in the world— the most "rationalized" secular humanist world imaginable is the empty one I have been describing, the place where there is only us and our creations. "We plow the fields and scatter / the good seed on the land. But it is fed and watered / by God's almighty hand. He sends the snow in winter / the warmth to swell the rain. The breezes and the sunshine / and soft refreshing rain." We are making the world a place where the voice of God is muffled. Not drowned out altogether—the evidence of God will still be seen in the kindness of humans for each other, in self-sacrificing love. But too often this kind of evidence is left for moments of epiphany; as daily reminders, nothing matches the sunrise and the rainfall. "All thy works with joy surround thee / Earth and heaven reflect thy rays." But do they? Or do they reflect our rays, our technology, our ways of life, our unwillingness to restrain ourselves. Aren't we on the verge of creating a place where humility is finally and completely replaced by pride? Aren't we on the verge of finally disconnecting deity from nature, from the one gut proof of the divine that has sustained countless people countless times? The problem with the greenhouse effect and with large scale genetic engineering is that they create a planet where God is mute—no sense insisting that God speaks from every blade of grass if it grows in a totally human-altered environment. It is too much to expect that we'll hear God speak from the moral equivalent of Astroturf. A clear lake speaks of many and glorious things; a polluted lake speaks only of man.

Perhaps it's just as well—perhaps we're merely getting rid of the last shreds of paganism and druidic nature worship. But that is not what my heart tells me. My heart tells me that the environmental destruction we see around us, if we allow it to continue, will be the prelude to a similar convulsive crisis of faith even more profound than the crises of faith that we have already experienced. When you live in a shopping mall where everything bears a human imprint, who do you worship? James Gustafson has written tellingly in recent years of a "theocentric" or God-centered ethics. Surely a life centered on God, not ourselves, is a goal of any religious seeking. But since God appears to few of us in tangible form, and since the pages of the theologians are not strong enough a foundation for many of us to erect our faith upon, building a God-centered life depends on the evidence of the divine we can find around us. Even when God spoke to Job he did not reveal himself: he revealed his works. It is theoretically possible to imagine a space-station world that speaks of the divine, but I think in practice the spirituality of such a world would soon become dry and empty, impossible to maintain. Even the most committed doubter, on the other hand, can often be shaken by the transcendent pleasure of sitting in a field of native flowers or standing on a wild beach. The sense of rightness, the intuition that the experience is more than the sum of its parts, is both profound and common. When such experiences begin to vanish (as the wildflowers grow less wild, and the beaches reflect our carbon emissions) their religious meaning will fade as well.

In some ways such a world would be the ultimate triumph of rationalism. In other ways, it would hold up to question the very idea of reason, as we pen ourselves in a sterile cell of our own invention. Such cataclysmic moments force us to face the most essential of questions: Why are we here? How *are* we to use our reason? It is easiest, of course, not to answer—to merely forge ahead as our momentum carries us. Or to answer with one of the orthodoxies supplied by each new generation of Job's friends. But as I have tried to demonstrate, our current orthodoxies have run out of steam—they can neither prevent devastating ecological harm, nor satisfy deeper needs. The orthodoxy of individual materialism and the cult of expansion have failed precisely because they insist on placing us at the center of everything, a role inappropriate both to our habitat and to our souls. Sometimes this is hard to see, for our orthodoxy has helped create our environments—what is a suburb but a physical manifestation of ease, unreality, and human-centeredness? What is a shopping mall but a television broadcast poured in concrete? That is one reason that the natural world is so important—it prods us to remember our place. And that is also, of course, a reason why it is so scary. I am reminded of a book by one of the ablest of John Muir's successors, the recently deceased Edward Abbey. In his classic *Desert Solitaire*, he describes one summer spent at Arches National Monument in Utah as a caretaker. This was in the days before they paved a road through it, and it became a kind of salt lick for the great wandering herds of Winnebagos. Back then it was pretty much deserted, and Abbey was alone with the rock and the wind. He recognized its beauty, but also its alienness. "The desert says nothing," he wrote. "Completely passive, acted upon but never acting, the desert lies there like the bare skeleton of Being, spare, sparse, austere, utterly worthless, inviting not love but contemplation. In its simplicity and order, it suggests the classical, except that *the desert is a realm beyond the human* and in the classicist view only the human is regarded as significant or even recognized as real." And of course Abbey was right. The desert is not for human beings—if it was there would be more water. Human beings have been able to settle it in large numbers only with the grossest intrusions on the workings of the natural world—the endless diversion of rivers and draining of aquifers, for instance. In another of his books, *The Monkey Wrench Gang*, Abbey writes about his reasons for trying to disrupt this destruction. His alter ego is hiking through the sand, along the proposed route of a new highway, pulling up all the orange surveyor's flags. He comes eventually to the stony rim of a small canyon and can see across on the other side the line of stakes marching on. "This canyon, then, was going to be bridged. It was only a small and little known canyon to be sure, with a tiny stream coursing down its bed, meandering in lazy bights over the sand, lolling pools under the acid green leafery of the cottonwoods falling over lip of stone into basin below, barely enough water even in spring to sustain a resident population of spotted toads, red-winged dragonflies, a snake or two, a few canyon wrens, nothing special." And yet Abbey demurred; his character knelt down and wrote "a message in the sand to all the highway construction contractors: Go home." This canyon, like so many other places, could only be paved over or left alone to no "constructive" end. Abbey chose leaving it alone; so, at least in the book of Job, did God, who makes it rain where there is no man.

Overcoming the orthodoxy that places us at the center is, I think, necessary not only for our individual souls, but also for the collective future of the churches. As I have tried to show, our faith, like our planet, is incompatible over the long run with any culture that puts people forever at its core and makes their material satisfaction its only goal. Standing up to that culture will not be in any sense easy—we are all participants in it, by the very time and place of our birth. For me, however, that imprinting has lessened slightly over the years as I have spent more time outdoors and more time in church. The church, because of its professed values, is the only institution left in society that has even, shall we say, a prayer of mounting a challenge to this dominant culture. And if it did I am convinced that it would be healthy not only for the environment but for the church. Because our message need not—should not—be only negative. It should be positive—replacing the ersatz joy of the consumer society with the real joy of God and creation. This, in a sense, is our ace in the hole. The consumer society has one great weakness, one flank left unprotected. And that is that for all its superficial sugary jazzy sexy appeal, it has not done a particularly good job of making people *happy*. It has left unsatisfied some basic human needs, or has tried to satisfy them inappropriately. There was a commercial for one brand of cosmetic airing the day I was watching television, and its punch line was, "Love you have to wait for. Pantene you can just go get." All things being equal, people would prefer love, I think. That we can offer. In the end, we need deeper answers to the deepest questions. Why are we here? At least in part, or so God implies in his answer to Job, to be a part of the great play of life, but only a part. We are not bigger than everything else—we are *like* everything else, meant to be exuberant and wild and *limited*. The very fact of the variety of life implies that—simple observation of the profusion around us should undermine our insistence on eternal primacy. Julian Barnes, in his magnificently irreverent novel *A History of the World in Ten and One Half Chapters*, describes the voyage of Noah's Ark from the viewpoint of a stowaway termite. The trip taught the animals a lot of things, he says, but "the main thing was this: that man is a very unevolved species compared to the animals. We don't deny, of course, your cleverness, your considerable potential. But you are, as yet at an early stage of your development. We, for instance, are always ourselves. That is what it means to be evolved. We are what we are, and we know what that is. You don't expect a cat suddenly to start barking, do you, or a pig to start lowing? But this is what, in a manner of speaking, [we] learned to expect from your species. One moment you bark, one moment you mew; one moment you wish to be wild, one moment you wish to be tame. We knew where we were with Noah only in this one respect: we never knew where we were with him."

But *what* part should we play? Even if we accept that our role is somehow to be limited, we know that our peculiar brains set us apart from the rest of creation. We have powers unique to ourselves; to refuse them would be like a bird refusing flight. Luckily, of course, there are whole huge categories of activity for which reason is utterly suited and which do not also spell destruction for the rest of the ecosystem. *Witnessing* the glory around us—that is a role no other creature can play. When God tells us we are created in his image, the only thing we know about God is that he finds creation beautiful—"Good. Very good." Perhaps that is a clue as to how we should see ourselves. Humans—the animal that appreciates. Appreciates each other, loves each other, protects each other from harm. Appreciates the rest of creation, loves the rest of creation, protects the rest of creation. These activities are deeply linked, of course—I have tried to show that any solution of our environmental problems is in large measure dependent on solving great numbers of social and political problems. Caring for the rain forest means caring for the Chinese means caring to ride bicycles means appreciating migratory songbirds means living mindful of the fourth generation down the road. All these are deeply human impulses, reflective of what is unique to our species. Most of our other accomplishments—huge dams, huge populations, huge abundance—are magnifications of the traits of all animals. They are uses of reason to do *better* than other creatures but not to do *different*. They reflect only a small percentage of the gifts we have been given as *humans*, and often they interfere with those gifts. Excessive materialism of the type deemed normal in Western societies clearly constitutes such an obstacle; so, even more, does the poverty of the developing world. You cannot fully exercise your unique human gifts—appreciation, witness, caring—when you are bowed down by hunger. The argument that we should free people to act as humans necessarily means, therefore, that we must address the deep economic chasm on this planet. The argument that the current approach of the industrialized countries is nearly as soul-deadening as the poverty of the South means that we must pull the sides of that chasm closer together, instead of trying to provide a bridge so that they can cross to our doubtful nirvana.

As Wendell Berry once asked in the title of an essay, "What are people for?" What feels most right to us? Find that and we will find the answers to what our place is, what our limits should be. And the answers, as I have said before, are paradoxical. We really want not utter individualism but a strong sense of community, not endless luxury but a large taste of the joy of service, not a totally packaged world but a reintroduction to the gorgeousness of the physical planet. The secret weapon of environmental change and of social justice must be this—living with simple elegance is more *pleasurable* than living caught in the middle of our consumer culture. What do I mean by simple elegance? There are a hundred examples, some of which I've already given: riding a bike or walking, so that you can hear your body again and feel the terrain; eating a simple diet, low enough on the food chain that you cause neither the environmental damage nor the arteriosclerosis promoted by our current menus; working less because you need less money which means someone else can share your job and you can reduce the stress and increase the satisfaction of your life; when nightfall comes, instead of turning on half the lights in the house and separating to the various television sets, lighting a candle or two and watching the sunset and talking or reading aloud. (It takes one power plant the size of Chernobyl simply to provide the continuous current that allows all our TV sets to turn on instantly when we flip the switch instead of taking a few seconds to warm up. But that is not the only drain from television—television is the constant stimulus of our desire for more stuff, and the constant wedge that prevents fellowship.) Many of us have spent time at retreat houses or monasteries, and sensed the peace that those experiences provide. But of course we're allowed to recreate that at home, to whatever extent we can. Many of us have experienced the pleasure that comes when there's a huge snowstorm in the winter and the power goes out for a day or two. Sure it's a nuisance, but it's also quiet—you can't drive and have to walk or ski. You gather with the neighbors, working and eating together. That experience too can be repeated, voluntarily, even in the middle of the summer. Instead of shopping at the supermarket for everything, we can grow more of our own food, and extra for our neighbors. Church communities provide natural places to organize some of these practices; if their members can be persuaded to try them, and if all we have been promised by God is true, then the satisfaction and joy of the experiment will begin to spread. We will find ourselves a little strengthened in the face of the vapid, empty culture we have created. That great laugh will start to spread, till with a chuckle and a shake of our heads we begin to turn our backs on the way we were and create new ways of being. We were born for community; we were born for service; we were born for joy; we were born to feel at home in this beautiful world; we were born to share certain unique gifts.

And of those gifts, the most unique and the most paradoxical is the ability to restrain ourselves. Conscious self-restraint belongs to no other creature, and for us it is the hardest of all tasks, both as individuals and as societies. Can we learn to genetically engineer plants and animals? Of course we can. Can we stop ourselves from genetically engineering plants and animals? Can we set strict limits, so that such work is okay for dealing with childhood diseases but taboo for anything else? Can we wean ourselves from cheap fossil fuel? Can we ignore the easy path? Can we muster the discipline to learn what we *really* want, and to follow that desire unwaveringly? When I said that this generation witnesses a confluence of thinking from atmospheric chemists and mystics, this is what I meant.

The easy answer, of course, is to say no. One of our current orthodoxies is to say that we are "destined" to behave in certain ways. Isn't human momentum forever forward, towards more control and power? Isn't it "human nature" to keep growing our economies forever, to reject a humbler approach to living our lives? I don't know the answer to that—no one does, because we've never made a concerted and society-wide effort. But I do think there is one at least mildly hopeful analogue, something that gives me some comfort. Fifty years ago, with World War II at its height, one could have made a convincing argument that people were destined to keep fighting ever larger and bloodier wars—certainly history would have supported such an argument. But then, at the end of the war, the atom bomb was exploded. In a way, this invention gave us all the Godlike power I have been describing today. It gave us the right to talk back to the God of Job, to say we had ultimate and total strength. J. Robert Oppenheimer, on witnessing the first explosion at Alamagordo, quoted from the Bhagavad Gita—"We are become Gods, destroyers of the worlds." But something interesting happened. So far, having that power, we have chosen not to exercise it. Indeed, and with ever increasing strength, we have built a taboo around this power. We still have wars, of course—too many wars, bloody wars, devastating and highly technological wars. But nuclear war, which many people expected in the early days of the Cold War, has become steadily more unthinkable.

One prays that this taboo will hold as nuclear weapons spread to new countries like North Korea or Iran. And it is not a perfect analogy. We have built this taboo because each of us can imagine what a nuclear explosion would be like and that imagining spurs us to act. The greenhouse effect, by contrast, results from a billion explosions of a billion pistons every second of every day around the world. Its impact is nearly invisible, much harder to build a myth around. Still the analogy gives me hope. With the atomic bomb a new physical fact came into the world, a fact so far-reaching that it is slowly changing the ways we conduct ourselves, leading us to greater restraint. And it was a new theological and philosophical fact as well—atomic war raised questions that conventional war never did. Even those comfortable with killing were queasy at the thought of such utter destruction—it seemed like more power than human beings could possibly justify, and so we have been slowly backing away from it. The greenhouse effect, and the other global environmental problems that we face, are new facts of the same magnitude. Already there are signs that people and nations around the world are ready to take on these facts. Not enough people, not the most powerful people—but there are enough of us that we've begun to constitute a force. Perhaps, just perhaps, in the mighty words of James Russell Lowell, new occasions will once more teach new duties, and time make ancient good uncouth.

And if we can teach ourselves those new duties, then the immense recuperative power of God's creation may be enough to erase at least the most horrible of our damage. I live, as I said, in the Adirondack mountains of upstate New York. The Adirondacks are among the oldest mountains on earth and eons ago they were the tallest. Time has slowly worn them away, but they are still impressive and remote. Twenty years after Lewis and Clark returned from the West, the tallest mountain in New York State, Mt. Marcy, still had not been climbed by a European. Once settlers came, however, they came with a vengeance. The streams were dammed for power; the hemlocks were stripped so that their bark could be used for tanning; most of all the loggers attacked the woods with amazing vigor. A hundred years ago, they were largely logged off—these remote mountains, the headwaters of the Hudson River, stripped bare of their pine and hemlock. But then some very visionary New Yorkers decided to preserve them. They carved out a six million-acre park, half public and half private, and amended the state constitution so that on the public land no tree could be cut again. It is a curious place, a rare hybrid of park and settlement—a true experiment in people living near nature. A century has not been enough to restore the primeval forest but it has been long enough to create again a true wilderness, the largest by far in the eastern United States. It is wild country—bear and coyote and mink and lynx. Out my back door you can wander through several hundred thousand acres of contiguous wilderness, land without road or cabin. It has revived, this land—it's a tremendously inspiring place, a symbol of what we might be able to do if we set our minds to it. And of what nature will do on its own, given half a chance. In the last decade, moose have begun to wander in again from the north and the east—an animal absent for a century is now taking up root again in these mountains. The first eagle chicks in nearly thirty years fledged in the park in the 1990s—and now there are dozens of nests on dozens of remote lakes. There is a re-creation going on—the world of the first chapter of Genesis is slowly reasserting itself, and many people are in fact doing their best to exercise responsible dominion over the land, to act as stewards. The state government has enacted some of the world's toughest land-use laws for the people who live in the Adirondacks. Forty-acre zoning is the rule for much of the park. You need special permits, granted only after environmental review, to make even small alterations to your home. Big projects, like golf courses, are routinely turned down. Not everyone likes it, but the voters of New York by and large continue to support the regulations—continue to say that at least in this special place the desire of human beings will not be the ultimate arbiter. It should be a model for much of the rest of the country and the world. I see each day that we do not face a hopeless task.

Merely a daunting one. It is always easier to cling to orthodoxy. Though the other world looks appealing, it is a trapeze swing away, and we fear. Often, I must be goaded to think, to realize, to try to grasp what is truly human. I was hiking in the hills behind my house last summer when I stepped on a hornet's nest. I was stung at least seventy times, and it hurt like nothing I have ever felt. And, alone, half an hour's hike from home, I was scared—I knew I was having some sort of reaction because hives were swelling across my chest. I have a good imagination, so it was not much of a stretch to believe that I might not make it back home. And yet the strongest feeling, as I ran back down the ridge, was a feeling of prayer—the simplest sort of prayer. Thank you God for those birds. Thank you God for these trees. Even, I think, thank you God for the hornets. Thank you that I am somehow linked to all of this. Never before had I felt quite so profoundly the rightness of the world around me—perhaps because it was my first experience as a potential link in the food chain. It was the least separated I had ever been, the closest to a creature. A trip to the hospital eventually erased my myriad bumps, but not the feeling of desperate at-homeness that I felt that afternoon. These reflections are largely an outgrowth of that stumble into the hornet's nest. If they draw from the book of Job any one lesson for our time, it is this: We need to stop thinking so much in terms of our "environment." An environment is a human creation: the home environment, the office environment. It counts—we need clean air and clean water, of course. But our environment is only a small part of something much larger. A planet, filled with the vast order of creation. It is a buzzing, weird, stoic, abundant, reckless, haunting, painful, perfect planet. All of it matters, all of it is glorious. And all of it can speak to us in the deepest and most satisfying ways, if only we will let it.